PENGUIN BOOKS

NO MORE BOSSES: THE JOURNEY TO SUSTAINABLE SELF-EMPLOYMENT

Adrian Tan is a self-employed Fractional Chief Marketing Officer (CMO), Future of Work influencer, HR tech consultant, and content creator based in Singapore. He helps HR companies in Southeast Asia to drive awareness, leads, and sales. He is the host of *The Adrian Tan Show*, where he interviews HR leaders and influencers on the future of work, and was the co-host of *Work It*, a work-related podcast by CNA. He has been featured as one of the top HR influencers in Asia and globally by various publications and platforms. Adrian writes regularly on CNA and his website: adriantan.com.sg.

T0369979

ADVANCE PRAISE FOR
NO MORE BOSSES

'I first met Adrian when he started writing work and career commentaries for CNA. I used to edit his raw copy and often laughed at the anecdotes he shared to make a point. Eventually, when I had to look for a co-host for a work podcast, I thought about him as my so-called partner-in-crime. If you heard him, Adrian sounds like someone you may have met during army, or in school or bumped into at the local hawker centre. Someone with solid, real-life experiences and the audacity to share them openly. What he has written in this book is no different. It's a pillar to post accounting of his very rich and varied life. A life that isn't like the cookie-cutter success story we see in a typical Singaporean. But a true accounting of life and work in all its richness.'

—Crispina Robert, Senior Editor at Mediacorp

'Some mistakes are necessary. But some others are extremely costly and can be paralyzing. The latter in the context of pursuing your self-employment path is what KILLS a lot of professionals embarking on this path. I know this well enough having quit my first and only job at twenty-eight years old and scaling my practice from a $50k per year one to a seven-figure business.

Adrian's book is written with a lot of grounded insights, practical value not just from his feature personalities and himself and my favourite segment—on brand building on LinkedIn. It's a good blend of big level paradigm shifts to the specific ground actions you have to take to ensure you can swim stronger and survive in the waves of business. It's also light-hearted enough to ensure you are not bogged down by a million and one to-dos or "inspirational nuggets". If you're ever contemplating quitting your job and having a "no boss lifestyle"—read this. You will have yourself to thank.'

**—Benjamin Loh, CSP (Agency Owner &
Growth Coach)**

'As the Founder and CEO of Kobe, I'm honoured to endorse *No More Bosses* by Adrian Tan, a game-changing read. To me, what sets this book apart is its celebration of vulnerability and "naive optimism"— which you will find in the book, making it a rare gem in a sea of cynical narratives.

No More Bosses transcends traditional self-help literature by emphasizing the importance of conquering oneself rather than others. It ingeniously merges self-help principles with practical guidance, making it a comprehensive guidebook for personal growth. What truly resonates with me are the realistic examples and case studies featuring everyday Singaporeans. By showcasing relatable stories, this book empowers readers to take actionable steps towards their dreams.

In a world saturated with tales of the already famous, *No More Bosses* stands out by spotlighting local Singaporean names, making success feel within reach for all. If you're seeking a refreshing take on empowerment and guidance, look no further than this transformative masterpiece.'

—Evangeline Leong, CEO, Kobe

'*No More Bosses* is a personal manifesto. Adrian knows the uncharted road ahead for a budding entrepreneur. Every page is born out of his own personal experience. He shares from the heart, taking the reader on well guided journey of being your own boss.

While going solo may be the dream of many, the first few steps forward can be daunting, even nerve-wrecking. I know how that feels, as Adrian and I both quit our jobs which we had held for two decades.

Just last year, I ventured out with a partner, and even roped in my wife for that extra confidence booster.

No More Bosses is a practical guide. The chapters on financial planning and forecasting, optimising productivity and achieving work-life balance, and brand positioning and setting marketing objectives will help one to keep his/her focus on what matters in the long run.

Adrian's manifesto is your grounded companion, as you stop living out the script of another, and write your own as your own boss.'

—Michael Han, Managing Partner at Han & Lu Law Chambers LLP

'Adrian is the boss! He is an inspiration to many mid-career switchers, truly embodying the "never say die" attitude. I have worked with him throughout his two years of life with *No More Bosses* and he has always been insightful and approachable as the "HR Influencer". Tips and tricks aside, the book dives deeper into how he reframed his mind over the course of intense changes and these mental exercises are complicated to say the least. I believe you will find great value through his vulnerable storytelling and the wisdom he has derived.'

—Reggie Koh, Chief Financial Coconut at The Financial Coconut

'In *No More Bosses: The Journey to Sustainable Self-Employment*, Adrian distils his journey in a way that took me back to my entrepreneurial journey. Honest, thought-provoking, and a stark contrast to the buzzword-filled options out there. It has everything I look for in a book—heart, a compelling story, and a strong sense of understanding what we need to hear. It is a must-read for entrepreneurs, business owners, or anyone who has gone through the rigours of being employed.'

—Chen Terng Shing, Founder of SYNC PR

'Adrian broke down the process of employment to self-employment in tangible, actionable steps. This book is a treasure trove of practice tips for anyone keen to explore the life of an entrepreneur, and embrace possibilities to reshape their mindsets and skill sets.'

—**Chuen Chuen Yeo, Managing Director,**
ACESENCE Agile Leadership
SG 40-over-40 Inspiring Women
Best Leadership Coach APAC Business Awards 24

'*No More Bosses* provides a pragmatic roadmap for navigating the transition from traditional employment to self-employment. This book distils that journey into actionable insights through real-life stories and practical tools. It demystifies the challenges and is an essential read, offering clarity and confidence to those ready to make the leap. *No More Bosses* is a testament to the courage it takes to leave the familiar behind and a reminder that the rewards of doing so can surpass our wildest expectations.'

—**Su-Yen Wong, Founder, Remarkable**
Reinventors Community

'If you are serious about self-employment, Adrian has got practical business and marketing concepts covered.

Sustainable self-employment requires the mindset of managing it like a business, for one. Adrian's book covers the fundamentals necessary for success.'

—**Derick Ng, CEO & Co-Founder, Clickr**

'As someone who's been self-employed for ten years, it's difficult to read this and not feel deeply understood.

Adrian makes the path to self-employment sound deceptively simple, while at the same time surfacing some hard truths about the journey in today's unique environment.

His writing is very relevant, humorous, and real. It gives the aspiring self-employed person all the tools to start and succeed.'

—**Eugene Cheng, Partner at HighSpark**

'Adrian Tan's *No More Bosses* is more than just a book; it's a manifesto for anyone feeling trapped in the relentless cycle of corporate life. Through his candid recount of personal tribulations and the ultimate journey to self-employment, Tan does not just share a story; he offers a lifeline. This book is a beacon of hope for those yearning to break free from the confines of traditional employment, illuminating a path towards autonomy and fulfilment.

Tan's narrative is both inspiring and instructional. He doesn't shy away from the harsh realities of making such a significant life change, especially in the challenging economic landscape of Singapore. His experiences, from confronting workplace bullying to navigating the complexities of personal branding in the corporate world, highlight the courage it takes to stand firm in one's values and the resilience required to forge a new path.

No More Bosses is a compelling read for anyone at a career crossroads. Tan's journey from resignation in a "blaze of glory" to embracing the uncertainties of self-employment underscores the importance of authenticity, perseverance, and adaptability. His story is a testament to the power of reclaiming one's career and life, making this book an essential guide for the modern professional seeking to escape the rat race and live on their own terms.'

—Rachele Focardi, Multigenerational Workforce Strategist CEO & Founder XYZ@Work

NO MORE MORE BOSSES

THE JOURNEY TO SUSTAINABLE
SELF-EMPLOYMENT

Adrian Tan

PENGUIN BOOKS

An imprint of Penguin Random House

PENGUIN BOOKS

Penguin Books is an imprint of the Penguin Random House group of
companies whose addresses can be found at
global.penguinrandomhouse.com

Published by Penguin Random House SEA Pte Ltd
40 Penjuru Lane, #03-12, Block 2
Singapore 609216

First published in Penguin Books by Penguin Random House SEA 2024

Copyright © Adrian Tan 2024

All rights reserved

10 9 8 7 6 5 4 3 2 1

The views and opinions expressed in this book are the author's own and the
facts are as reported by him which have been verified to the extent possible,
and the publishers are not in any way liable for the same.

ISBN 9789815233131

Typeset in Garamond by MAP Systems, Bengaluru, India

This book is sold subject to the condition that it shall not, by way of trade
or otherwise, be lent, resold, hired out, or otherwise circulated without the
publisher's prior consent in any form of binding or cover other than that in
which it is published and without a similar condition including this condition
being imposed on the subsequent purchaser.

www.penguin.sg

For everyone who dreams of quitting and being their own boss

My boss told me to go home early. Then the phone rang: "Come back! I changed my mind!"
—*Anonymous*

Contents

Part III: Launching Your Self-Employment Venture

Part IV: Emotional Resilience and Motivation

Prologue

My Journey to Self-Employment

Well, I did it—I finally quit after twenty years and countless jobs! And let me tell you, it felt so liberating to say those words. It was like a huge weight had been lifted off my shoulders. The relief was palpable after being stuck on the corporate hamster wheel for so long.

The final straw? A LinkedIn post about workplace bullying hit close to home, triggering memories of my own experiences of being bullied as a kid. I voiced support for the issue in the comments. But the next thing I know, my boss wants me to delete my comment because the company implicated was a partner of ours.

I refused to back down or censor my perspective. From there, tensions escalated rapidly. One thing led to another, and soon I found myself resigning in a blaze of glory.

It was a bridge burnt, no going back. But I had spoken my truth, even if it cost me my job. I was finally free of a toxic culture muzzling my voice.

Of course, the reality of needing a new source of income soon sank in. The job search kicked off swiftly during my notice period. With over fifteen years of experience in HR tech, I was confident fresh opportunities would surface quickly.

I got shortlisted for final round interviews at two promising HR tech firms. However, a startling red flag emerged in one of the interviews. They expressed concern over my growing 'influencer status' in the HR space stemming from my prolific writing and content.

This flagged that censorship issues could repeat in any structured corporate role due to my personal brand. I was now seemingly unemployable—my perspective too unfiltered for 'politically correct' companies.

With no appealing corporate prospects, I decided to go solo again, but without managing others this time. Been there, done that, both in my own business and others'—I'd had enough unpredictable people management drama!

Self-employment where I don't have to deal with workplace emotions sounded perfect. Just focus on the work, not babysitting egos.

Today marks nearly two years into this roller-coaster journey, navigating the midlife self-employment path here in wildly expensive Singapore. Let me tell you, doing this mid-career with financial obligations feels like playing on hard mode!

Risk aversion has definitely kicked in more with age compared to twenties entrepreneurial daring. Mortgage payments and family duties make you less prone to recklessness.

I've certainly made my share of mistakes along the way. But learning from failures is all part of the experience. The euphoric successes, freedom, and sense of purpose have made all the ups and downs worthwhile.

Through it all, I've remained optimistic, thanks to the resilience built from previous business attempts. I'm determined to make this work without everything crumbling around me in the process.

My hope is that readers can benefit from the raw lessons and experiences I share here. Use them to plan your own escape from the rat race, if done thoughtfully.

You see, if I can pull off this mid-career pivot to self-employment in wildly expensive Singapore as an average guy, others can do it, too, with the right mindset and pragmatic preparations.

And that's really what this book is all about—helping you take control to liberate your career so you can live life on your own terms!

Part I

Leaving the Corporate World Behind

Chapter 1

Cubicle Jailbreak: My Winding Road to Self-Employment

'The only way to do great work is to love what you do. If you haven't found it yet, keep looking. Don't settle.'

—Steve Jobs

The year was 2000. As a fresh-faced twenty-one-year-old Singaporean lad having just completed my mandatory two-year military service, securing a corporate job seemed like an inevitable and exciting next step. Like most of my peers graduating at that time, I dreamed of climbing the corporate ladder to one day attain the markers of success—the '5Cs' of cash, car, credit card, condo, and country club membership.

Never mind that I had barely scraped through secondary school and even spent a month in military prison for recklessly overturning an army vehicle during a late-night joyride (but that's a story for another day). In my youthful naivety, I was convinced I could overcome my lacklustre academic record and chequered past through hard work and determination in the corporate world.

Landing my first job felt like a huge achievement already, considering I had no university degree to speak of, having only completed my O levels. Through a recruiter's referral, I secured a customer service role at an upstart telecommunications company that was launching to challenge incumbent. The grand starting pay of $1,050 per month plus generous commissions and allowances felt like a fortune to my young self.

This was my chance to prove myself and make up for my lack of qualifications, I thought. I may have stumbled in my formal education, but I resolved to pour my heart and soul into excelling in this first real job.

As a new recruit in a call centre team of mostly older and more experienced agents, I took it upon myself to learn everything about the role as quickly as possible. When our antiquated computer systems crashed constantly, I discovered a skill for swiftly flipping through the printed Yellow Pages directories to find customer numbers and other information they needed. My teammates were amazed at how I could locate obscure listings in seconds.

Before long, my resourcefulness, tireless work ethic, and rapport with customers caught the attention of management. Within just three months, I was offered the opportunity to undergo supervisor training as part of the first batch for the call centre.

I could barely contain my excitement and sense of achievement. At just twenty-one, I was being groomed for a management role! This felt like vindication and a turning point in my life—a chance to finally put my history of academic failures and youthful misdeeds firmly behind me.

Or so I thought.

In hindsight, I was wholly unprepared for the responsibilities of being a supervisor at such a tender age. Like Icarus flying too close to the sun, the taste of authority soon went straight to my head. I started throwing my new-found weight around, delighting in being able to boss my teammates around for a change.

Many of them were not much older than I was but had been working for longer. Sensing an opportunity, a couple of them started asking me to clock them in when they showed up late or not at all. Eager to be seen as the 'cool' boss, I agreed to help cover for them by fudging their attendance records.

In my naive head, I convinced myself this was just an innocuous thing that would smooth over our working relationship. I kept rationalizing that it would just be a one-time favour, a little white lie that wouldn't happen again.

Suffice to say, things quickly snowballed as word got around. Requests to doctor the attendance logs became more brazen and frequent. Teammates who were once punctual started showing up late or skipping work without reason, knowing I would have their back.

Like a passive parent unable to discipline unruly children, I had allowed myself to become a doormat, afraid to put my foot down. Until inevitably, the sham was busted during a surprise management audit. We were all promptly hauled up and given stern formal warnings, with my supervisor title unceremoniously revoked. I was demoted and sent back to the floor as a regular call centre agent.

What stung even more than the humiliation of being stripped of my promotion was knowing I had no one to blame but myself. In just six short months, I had dug myself into a hole again, throwing away a golden opportunity through my poor decisions fuelled by youth and inexperience. It was a bitter pill to swallow.

My zeal for the job evaporated instantly. I kept my head down, avoided the colleagues I had let down, and quietly rode out the remaining one year of my contract without extension. My boss' parting words continued ringing in my ears—'I hope you have learned your lesson.'

As 2001 approached, I made a resolution to start afresh. The dotcom frenzy was taking off in a big way globally. Seduced by glistening visions of relaxed work cultures with beanbags, arcade rooms, and free snacks, I jumped at the chance to join an upstart dotcom start-up in the online education space. They had managed to raise a substantial amount of venture capital (VC) funding and set up a swanky office in Singapore's Central Business District (CBD).

Compared to the regimented atmosphere and pressure-cooker environment of the telco call centre, this felt like a breath of fresh air. I thrived in the informal, energetic vibe among the young pioneers disrupting the status quo. There was a real sense of mission that our work could shape the future of education in Singapore and beyond.

For close to a year, I genuinely enjoyed my role as a customer support executive, resolving login issues, fixing bugs, and liaising with schools on adoption of the platform. I had found redemption after stumbling early in my first job.

Or so I thought, yet again.

Barely a year later, the dotcom bubble went spectacularly bust. The company's funding dried up as investors grew wary. Within two weeks, over 75 per cent of the staff were abruptly retrenched, including myself. The glitzy office was shuttered and only a skeletal team remained.

As I stood with my box of belongings outside the office that final day, I could scarcely believe my awful luck. It was like a recurring nightmare—twice now within my first two jobs, opportunities that appeared promising had been ripped away without warning.

Was I doomed to go through my entire career this way, with constant instability and getting the short end of the sticks? That lingering thought haunted me as I struggled to come to terms with having to start my job search all over again.

With a bruised ego and rock-bottom confidence, I felt I possessed the opposite of the Midas touch—everything I touched went up in flames. But time to gloat is a luxury afforded for the wealthy, and that was not me. Trying my best to push the recent bad experiences to the back of my head, I opened up my browser and started sending fresh job applications to job openings that might appreciate my skill sets. Before long, a recruitment company responded. Their client was a distributor for aviation spare parts and they had an opening for a customer service executive. Two interviews later, I got an offer.

By the time I joined my third company, my mindset had grown rather jaded and cynical. I no longer bought into lofty corporate values or promises of growth and opportunity. I had learned the hard way that fancy credentials and rhetoric could disappear in an instant when business conditions changed.

This company distributed aircraft spare parts and was far removed from the high-flying dotcom world—just solid, no-frills work. I fit well into the structured, predictable environment and my role as a customer service executive coordinating orders from regional airlines.

For close to a year, I finally started feeling settled and cautiously optimistic that I had found stability. My boss took notice of my diligence and strong work ethic, promising me promotion opportunities down the road.

Or so I thought, for the third time.

In early 2003, just as I was getting comfortable, SARS emerged and changed everything. The virus outbreak centred in Hong Kong and Southern China brought air travel to its knees almost overnight. Airlines stopped flying routes to affected regions and new bookings dried up.

Our airline customers in Taiwan, Hong Kong, and Korea drastically cut orders for spare parts as entire fleets were grounded. As the sole breadwinner for my family then, I could scarcely sleep at night, anxiety-ridden about losing yet another job.

The company directors tried to reassure us that it was only temporary, that we just had to hunker down and weather the storm together. But their solemn faces betrayed the gravity of the situation. A week later, the managing director resigned unexpectedly.

That was the proverbial writing on the wall. Having experienced two abrupt lay-offs before, I knew in my gut that the company was in dire straits. *Am I going to score a hat-trick in getting retrenched?* That thought kept gnawing at me every waking minute.

Needing an outlet, I caught up with my friends from high school to banter. It was then that I realized I was not the only victim of the economic climate. It also affected one of my friends, Ryan, who had spent his career so far in the structured cabling industry.

Just the previous year, he too had faced retrenchment as economic conditions kept worsening. Eventually, together with another high school senior who was in the same department, they decided 'enough was enough'. If companies were so quick to cut jobs to save their own skin, why not be their own bosses and take fate into their own hands?

And so the two of them had cobbled together their limited savings and started their own structured cabling business. They used a small apartment and turned it into a makeshift office. Business was still slow, but they were surviving.

Ryan invited me to swing by their 'office' sometime to take a look. I took him up on the offer the very next day, partly curious and also badly needing any sliver of hope during this low point.

Stepping into that cramped apartment that was their operational hub, I was greeted by a scene of organized chaos. Tools, ladders, and spools of cable lined the walls. Stacks of papers and blueprints were strewn across the floor.

An odd feeling washed over me as I watched Ryan and his partner, Stephen, deftly navigating the obstacle course of their making. Rather than a mess, what I observed was a hive of relentless activity and progress. There was a vital, energetic spirit about them that I had not felt in a long time.

In between coordinating schedules and sourcing supplies, they shared more about the thrills and challenges of being new entrepreneurs. The risk and uncertainty sounded terrifying to me, but so did the freedom and agency they now possessed. No more office politics or corporate red tape to adhere to. They controlled their own fates now for better or worse.

A spark ignited within me as I listened to them. These were two ordinary guys very much like myself, who had been knocked down repeatedly but refused to stay down. They possessed no special skills or advantages that I did not have myself. If they could take that leap into entrepreneurship, what was stopping me?

The siren call of entrepreneurship was like a forbidden fruit dangling within reach. I just had to take a bite and seize my own destiny once and for all.

Filled with nervous excitement, I decided to take the plunge while I still had the youth and hunger to see it through. At twenty-four, with minimal financial commitments, it seemed like the right time to roll the dice. If these next few years proved that entrepreneurship was not suitable for me, at least I could return to employment in the future with no regrets about never trying.

With $6,000 of seed capital borrowed from my mother, I bit the bullet and registered a recruitment agency start-up with Ryan and two other friends from university. We operated out of a shared shophouse rental in Tanjong Pagar to conserve costs. That was how RecruitPlus started.

I will not sugar-coat it—those early years were bruising and tumultuous. We made every rookie mistake possible, from cashflow issues to underestimating costs to hiring the wrong people at the wrong time. Several times, the business teetered on the brink of bankruptcy and I considered throwing in the towel.

But the fire in my belly to prove I could make it kept burning. The fear of failure and returning to a life of uncertainty as an employee drove me to work crazy hours and fight on through tears and self-doubt. There was no safety net to fall back on any more—it was do or die trying.

Against the odds, we managed to slowly stabilize the business. My previous jobs had provided valuable insights into sales, customers, and people management that I was able to apply even as a novice entrepreneur. I learned to play to our strengths while outsourcing our shortcomings.

Year by gruelling year, we increased our revenue, expanded the team, and carved out a modest niche serving SMEs and MNCs hiring across various industries. By 2004, we had moved out of the shared office into our own space. By 2009, we had expanded to fourteen employees and cracked the million-dollar revenue mark.

After eleven long years, we had built the company up to a point where I felt comfortable selling my stake to existing shareholders and making my first exit. It was by no means an overnight success story, but through blood, sweat, and tears, we had gotten there in the end.

I had made my point—not just to the world, but to myself. Almost fifteen years since leaving school, I had finally overcome the self-limiting beliefs about my ability to be successful in my career. The fires of ambition still raged within me. But at thirty-five, with a wife and three young kids at home, my priorities had evolved.

My time was no longer wholly mine to spend building businesses. My energy had limits compared to my younger days. Perhaps it was time to trade the uncertainties and demands of managing a small business and consider something more manageable.

Just before my exit, I had co-written a career guidebook with a fellow headhunter. That book became a calling card for us to deliver keynote addresses and even training workshops.

Could this be the mark of my next thing? I quickly incorporated CareerLadder and that became my entity to market myself as a career coach. I went about providing one-to-one coaching session and occasionally at a larger scale for corporations such as WSG, e2i, and even corporate workshops for James Cook University and AIA.

But despite all that, the business was just not sustainable for the financial obligations I was under. Reality called for a higher and more regular income. With some lucky timing, an opportunity to join a private education institution as a full-time talent management manager came along. It felt like the perfect role and company to transition into after running my own recruitment business.

After twelve years of gritty, hand-to-mouth bootstrapping, the perks and polish of corporate life held strong appeal again. A stable income, additional workplace benefits, being able to disconnect after work hours—these were boons I had taken for granted during my entrepreneurship journey.

Most seductively, it presented the chance to step off the roller coaster for a while and rekindle the professional ambitions I had placed on the back-burner while building my company. I saw a clear path to rising up the corporate ladder again by leveraging the skills I had honed as an entrepreneur.

The pivot back to employment off the heels of my entrepreneurial chapter was going to be the next act in my career journey. Or so I thought. Again!

Just two days into my new job, I learned about the weekly sales meeting that I had to attend. It was scheduled for Tuesday/Wednesday, so I asked for clarification on the exact day and time to be ready and prepared.

'The meeting lasts for two days.'

What?

For the following weeks, I spent 40 per cent of my work time in endless meetings. They had no clear agenda, just a long-winded lecture from the COO. He believed this was the way to boost the business. The record was two and a half days. The next day, one of the sales directors quit. I followed suit shortly after.

The company was run by a know-it-all CEO and a clueless COO. Working there was anything but fulfilling. Even though I had sold my first business, most (if not all) of the proceeds went towards paying off my debt. Financially, I was back to square one.

So I had to look for other opportunities and came across a new outplacement agency that was opening in Singapore. They needed someone to lead the Singapore office and had experience in recruitment and career coaching.

That sounded like me!

I quickly jumped on the bus that I thought would take me to my destination. But before I could even settle in, I was thrown under the bus. The project was based on unrealistic projections from the HQ. It was up to the ops team to meet those numbers. And it was a huge challenge. The goal was to help the main government agency place unemployed Singaporeans back into the job market.

But we only got the difficult cases that the agency couldn't handle themselves. We were one of the two vendors that they outsourced to. That made closing the cases harder and financially unsustainable. We only got paid for each successful placement. And we had to prove it with paper evidence. But most of the candidates ghosted us after getting their jobs.

No evidence, no money.

To save face, someone had to take the blame. And that was me.

It was devastating. I had high hopes of making this work. I worked harder than I did for my own business. I resorted to chain smoking and drinking to cope with the stress. When I got the news, I was in a shock for the rest of the day. My mind flashed back to the time when I worked at the dotcom and I was at the mercy of the organization.

It felt like the horror movie *Final Destination*—no matter what I did, the outcome was always the same.

Still without a financial cushion to support me and my family, I had to keep grinding along the corporate path. The final straw came a few years later. And there were two of them.

My last corporate job was with a quasi-government HR certification body that clashed with my entrepreneurial spirit. Ten months into the job, my ex-boss saw a LinkedIn comment I made to support a friend who was a victim of corporate bullying.

He told me to take down my comment because the bully was from another quasi-government body. Having been a victim myself when I was a kid, I refused. After a long and heated argument, I said for the first time to another person: 'I quit.'

The office politics within the organization had already stretched me thin. It didn't take much to make me snap.

The next day, I wondered: *Now what?*

I still didn't have the financial runway I thought I needed to escape the corporate rat race. It seemed like I had no choice but to look for another job. But I decided to stick with the private sector from now on.

The private sector seemed like the better option. I put the word out and I secured two job interviews with a couple of HR tech companies. I passed the second round with the CEO in the first one and I was scheduled to speak with the CMO in the second one.

I thought I had it all figured out. I was confident that I could land a job from either of the two HR tech companies while I served my notice period.

Take that, ex-boss!

But then I heard a statement from the CMO interviewer from the second HR tech company that changed everything.

I had built a strong online presence by writing about various work-related topics—from hiring to job search, to HR tech, and more. I had a large following on my website, podcast, and my commentaries on Channel NewsAsia (CNA).

At the time of this writing, I had close to 40,000 followers on LinkedIn, and I had received accolades from the media as one of the top HR influencers of 2023.

The interviewer knew about my HR influencer status. And he was worried about it. I wasn't completely surprised, as the former GM who arranged the interview had mentioned this concern to me before. But it still caught me off guard when he said it to my face.

He had valid reasons to be concerned. There could be reputational risks if I posted content that was controversial or problematic. The messaging could also clash with the corporate branding.

It was like playing with fire. It could be useful and beneficial, but it could also cause damage and destruction. I could already picture my days if I joined this company. It was a red flag for me and the last straw.

I had had enough. I didn't need a financial runway to quit the corporate nonsense. It was time to awaken the twenty-four-year-old in me who had jumped off the cliff into the entrepreneurial abyss and built the plane on the way down.

But I also realized that I was no longer twenty-four. I was forty-two then. Did I really want to go through the entrepreneurial grind and neglect my kids in the process? Even if I could overcome that, I would have to hire people and manage them. And that was not my forte.

Maybe I could give solopreneurship another try. I had experimented with that right after my recruitment business. A career guide book that I had co-authored led to training and coaching gigs that I had tried to capitalize on. But maybe not as a career coach, as that business model just didn't work here in Singapore.

It was thrilling and terrifying. I was an overthinker and I had mastered that skill as I aged. Even though I knew deep down this was the right path for me, I hardly knew where to start. I remembered people telling me that marketing was my superpower. Maybe I could lean into that and see where it took me?

I had already secured two adjunct teaching assignments and I put out a LinkedIn post in the evening about going independent and inviting any collaboration opportunities. With a huge sigh, I closed my laptop and hoped for the best.

Twenty-four hours later, the unimaginable happened.

Three different companies contacted me to discuss engaging my service. I did content for two of them and became a fractional CMO for the third. I established Marketing Sumo, a private limited company specifically designed to tackle the invoicing and tax complexities of freelance life. This clean separation allowed me to focus on exceeding expectations, and my income soared—twice of what I used to make!

I should have done this sooner!

Today, I have two retainers—one in content, which is my first and longest client, and one as a fractional CMO for another. On top of that, my personal podcast endeavours caught the attention of CNA when they wanted to do their own show about work matters. I am still the co-host of that podcast.

Occasionally, I get approached to write articles, speak, or teach and these form the most erratic part of my income.

Even though I wish I had done this sooner, it was perhaps only at that moment that the stars aligned for me. And I don't mean that in a superstitious way where things are controlled by fate and horoscope.

The market perception of me has evolved compared to the days of career coaching in 2005. Coupled with a better business model, it was almost an effortless overnight pivot made possible with decades of unconscious prep work.

So what exactly is the key appeal behind self-employment?

To answer that, I dug deeper into my stories as well as the stories of other former corporate hamsters. I will also be touching on aspects of self-employment at different levels. Whether you are sitting on the fence as you ponder if self-employment may be right for you, or perhaps you are already committed but unsure of how to go about marketing yourself and your business, subsequent chapters have these topics covered. These are tried-and-tested paths I took, knowingly and accidentally, to arrive where I am today. The chapters are all independent so feel free to jump ahead depending on the stage you are at right now.

I hope my experiences and mistakes, from which I learned, would pave the way for your version of no more bosses.

Key Takeaways

- Given the unstable early career such as getting laid off from two jobs in a row due to economic downturns (and almost scoring a hat trick with the third) led me to seriously consider self-employment as an alternative path.
- Visiting friends who had taken the leap to start their own business showed me that entrepreneurship was a viable option, and one where you have more control over your future success or failure.
- Deciding to take the plunge and starting a recruitment agency with partners, which involved many struggles in the early years, helped me gain invaluable business experience over eleven years of growing the company.
- Any attempts to return to corporate jobs never seemed to work out in the long run as I faced issues like unrealistic expectations, lack of flexibility due to politics, and bureaucracy.
- Realizing my skills and experience could be better leveraged as a freelance consultant, I decided to start my own solo consulting business, which has found success by marketing my expertise as an HR influencer and building clients. This allows me more freedom and a higher income potential.

Chapter 2

Signs It's Time to Make the Leap

'The journey of a thousand miles begins with a single step.'
—Lao Tzu

The smoke lingered from my twentieth cigarette of the day, the final wisp escaping before I crushed the empty pack under my palm. It was a ritual, the symbolic punctuation to another marathon session at the outplacement agency I'd joined. This was the third job I had since exiting from my recruitment business.

As the familiar sting of resignation washed over me, I knew this chapter, too, was nearing its end. This time, though, the prospect didn't bring the usual bittersweet closure. A glimmer of something new, something uncertain, flickered at the edge of my vision. This chapter wouldn't just signal the end of a dead-end job; it would mark the start of something unknown, a step into the void

Burnout and Health Impacts

When I first joined the outplacement agency, I was energized. Running the Singapore office provided a sense of purpose missing from my string of unsatisfying jobs post the recruitment business.

But as time progressed, realities set in. We were expected to closely follow HQ's playbooks, even when the directives didn't

fit local needs. This required building new programmes from
scratch through trial and error.

Unfortunately, HQ's targets increased exponentially each
month. And we became the dumping ground for the most
challenging cases, making achieving our KPIs a Sisyphean task.

As Timothy Ferriss tweeted in early January 2022, 'Being
busy is most often used as a guise for avoiding the few critically
important but uncomfortable actions' (Ferriss, 2021). This
constant busyness left me exhausted and overwhelmed.

I could feel my health deteriorating from the mounting stress.
While not a real coping mechanism, smoking provided respite
from the daily grind. My pack-a-day habit increased along with
my headaches.

If this sounds familiar, I'm not surprised. Per a Cigna study,
over 90 per cent of Singaporean workers experience burnout
(Cigna, 2022).

My friend Jaslyn Ng, a former corporate director, had a
similar experience. Though her asthma subsided after childhood,
it returned working long hours spanning the US and Singapore
time zones (Ng, 2022). As Greg McKeown captures in *Essentialism*
(McKeown, 2014), 'As demands and options multiply, we feel
overloaded, overworked, and overwhelmed.' This was our reality.

When Jaslyn's child fell ill, being absent during the
hospitalization was the final straw. Despite signing an attractive
offer of a quarter million per annum, Jaslyn resigned to become a
self-employed financial adviser.

She and I may seem like outliers but there are so many other
examples that I kept coming across.

A friend of mine was the head of data science at a local bank.
Due to resource constraint, he was wearing close to seven hats
at his work and the stress was almost too much to bear. The
volcano finally erupted. When he checked into the hospital, he
could barely walk. He was hospitalized for almost a month due to

exhaustion and burnout. Even though he was welcome to return to the company after his recovery, he decided otherwise.

Similar situation surrounds an acquaintance who is the executive director of a membership body. After three years in the stressful role, his medical prognosis shows high blood pressure and higher heart palpitations.

I also realized a commonality between all four of us. We hold significant positions in the management with higher responsibilities and are in the mid-career stage of our lives. When we are younger, mentally and biologically we are able to take whatever life throws at us. And given that this is during the early stages of our career, we won't get something that's too overwhelming thrown in our way.

But as we grow older, we become just like an older car. You can't use the argument that an older car should be able to drive faster than a new one because it has more road experience. We also need to account for wear and tear. And most of these occur with age which is beyond our physical control.

Saying 'no' today, when things start getting intense, prevents the need to say 'no' permanently to my career tomorrow. But more on that later.

Lack of Autonomy

Burnout isn't the only pitfall of traditional employment. The lack of autonomy also chafed me.

I still vividly recall the stinging disappointment at my first job in the telco call centre when my manager rejected my appeal for a second chance after my supervisory failure. Her swift dismissal slammed the door on any redemption arc.

Contrast that with the unbridled possibility that struck during a serendipitous coffee chat a few years later. As my friends shared their misery working for others, a lightbulb sparked—why not start our own recruitment business?

Our collective corporate experience tallied zero years in recruitment and none of us had ever managed a business. Had we sought permission to pursue this pipe dream, our own doubts would have torpedoed it.

But the beauty of entrepreneurship is permission isn't needed from gatekeepers. The authorities bless you with a license and the rest is up to you. No begging required.

This freedom from rules emboldened us to take the leap, even if Singapore's prevalent 'No U-Turn Syndrome' suggested the odds were stacked against us. We jumped in feet first, hustling our old employers for job openings to build up our portfolio. As days turned to weeks, and weeks to months, our baby steps slowly transformed an idea hatched over kopi into a thriving enterprise driving millions in annual recruitment revenue.

None of this would have happened if we had sought permission first.

But in traditional employment, everything funnels through gatekeepers up on high. Whether it is budget for a new project, headcount for your team, or cancelling a useless initiative, you are trapped lobbying others for a yes. Too often, the answer disappoints.

This lack of autonomy grinds you down over time. No wonder professionals, like the Cigna study highlighted, feel their corporate roles lack purpose.

Meaningless Work

The utter tedium of my days at my last corporate job first opened my eyes to the concept of 'bullshit jobs' coined by anthropologist David Graeber. In his 2018 book *Bullshit Jobs: A Theory*, he argues that millions toil away at meaningless roles they can't justify the existence of, yet pretend there's a reason for those.

These differ from bad jobs that are hard or poorly paid but still useful. Graeber outlined five types of bullshit jobs, from box tickers creating the illusion of productivity to taskmasters generating unnecessary work. He traces this phenomenon to cultural factors that equate jobs with self-worth.

Recent studies validate the theory, with 19 per cent of employees feeling their work lacks social value. Jobs in admin, sales, and business/finance are perceived as especially unnecessary.

I witnessed bullshit jobs first-hand while scrolling through laughable 'Day in the Life' TikToks at tech firms, depicting at most one to two hours of real work buffered by indulgence. My own corporate role had that essence. With no clear mandate beyond generating ignored papers, my hours stretched endlessly ahead, devoid of purpose.

Unlike my marketing or podcasting work today, that job lacked practical value and business feasibility. As studies show, such superfluous roles sap creativity and well-being.

I still shudder remembering the eerie quiet I witnessed while walking into the office during lockdown as the sole person on-site. The team wisely worked from home while I haunted the office searching for ways to fill the endless days.

In stark contrast, the autonomy of self-employment lets me devote my energy to assignments that truly help clients and listeners. Trading meaningless box-ticking and bureaucracy for real impact aligns work with meaning.

Rather than live to work at a large corporation, I now work to live serving my own small enterprise. The difference is night and day—purpose transforms work from a grinding chore into an intrinsic motivator.

My corporate bullshit job taught me to cherish work with tangible value. Chasing fancy titles loses appeal when you realize prestige often signifies nothing. I'd choose to be an indie marketer or podcaster over a prestigious sham role any day.

Bad Bosses

When I was promoting my recruitment business, I commissioned a now-defunct local YouTube channel to do a couple of videos for us. One of them was titled 'Top 10 types of Horrible Bosses' and it went viral very quickly.

Although it was tongue-in-cheek, it was extremely relatable as many of us have seen versions of them in real life. It may be funny as a viewer but you won't find it laughable if you actually have to work for a bad boss.

This is aligned with the findings in the Gallup report (Gallup, 2017). Respondents were asked the reasons why they quit their managers. Some of the reasons include:

- Lack of support, feedback, recognition, or guidance from their managers.
- Poor communication, trust, or rapport with their managers.
- Mismatch of expectations, goals, or values with their managers.
- High stress, burnout, or pressure from their managers.

One of my worst bosses was someone who is extremely fickle in decision-making. His master strategy is as fluid as water but not in the good way that Bruce Lee intended.

This was with an enterprise HR tech company and I was part of marketing for Southeast Asia. While strategizing for the Singapore market on Monday, we were unexpectedly tasked with prioritizing the Philippines by Wednesday. This abrupt shift, coupled with our leader's reliance on a global playbook less relevant to the local context, proved to be a significant challenge.

Another boss I had was clearly ill-suited for his position, which he held for nearly six years. An extreme introvert, he was often isolated in his corner office, leading many to believe he wasn't even in the office. However, constant communication and relationship building are essential tools for any good leader, regardless of their personal preferences.

This proved detrimental to the organization, which, despite having only forty employees, suffered from a high attrition rate.

This eventually prompted the board of directors to engage an HR consultancy at a cost of $36,000.

The consultancy conducted interviews and compiled a report, revealing troubling insights. During the subsequent board meeting, one director pointedly asked why the boss hadn't simply spoken to the employees himself—after all, there were only forty of them. This question highlighted the disconnect between the leader's isolation and the organization's needs.

While the boss certainly deserves criticism for his leadership style, I believe the ultimate responsibility lies with the higher-ups who placed him in such a crucial role. This is best explained by Dr Laurence J. Peter who conceptualized the Peter Principle in his 1976 book of the same title (Raymond Hull, 1976).

Dr Peter stated in his book that an employee's inability to fulfil the requirements of a given position that they are promoted to may not be the result of general incompetence on the part of the employee as much as it is due to the fact that the position simply requires different skills than those the employee actually possesses.

Imagine promoting a talented chef to head the research and development team of a new restaurant. While their culinary skills are impressive, they may lack the knowledge and creativity needed to develop innovative dishes. Similarly, promotions based solely on rule-following skills can overlook crucial qualities needed for policy creation.

We see this all too often: the top salesperson promoted to the top job in the organization. Sales is often the easiest role to measure in any profit-driven business, and its impact on the bottom line is undeniable. Additionally, sales positions often allow for easier overachievement compared to back-office operations. This success is often overemphasized, leading companies to promote star performers to roles that represent a step up but require a different, unvalidated skillset.

I witnessed this first-hand during my time in the recruitment industry. Top billers (top-performing recruiters) were routinely earmarked for supervisory, team leader, or managerial positions. However, the skills that made them excel in sales were often insufficient for their new roles. They were essentially thrown into the fire unprepared, leading to struggles and disillusionment.

My former boss, for example, transitioned from HR to become the CEO of an HR certification body. While his HR knowledge was valuable, the organization functioned more as a small business than an HR department. It would have been more effective to bring in someone with strong business acumen and then provide them with specific training on HR certification.

Unfortunately, these 'human chess moves' often remain opaque to employees caught in the corporate web. While not inherently bad, some bosses may be oblivious to the potential pitfalls of promoting individuals based solely on past performance in unrelated roles. Others may simply be adhering to outdated corporate norms, unaware of the need for more nuanced and individualized development strategies.

By shedding light on this issue and highlighting the consequences of poor promotion decisions, we can encourage a shift towards a more thoughtful and deliberate approach to leadership development. This requires not only a focus on past successes but also a careful evaluation of the skills and experience necessary for success in the new role. Ultimately, this shift will benefit both individual employees and the organizations they serve.

Lack of Freedom

Beyond just the potential of working under and dealing with a bad boss, there is another thing that I feel gnaws at you far more often. And that is getting permission to do what you truly wish to do.

My first visceral experience of lost freedom came during National Service after my carefree childhood days filled with hoops and video games. Overnight, I was plunged into a regimented world of regimented timetables and shared quarters with strangers.

Weekdays allowed time for either bodily functions or rest, never both. I began a countdown calendar when eighteen months of service remained, gaining assurance from ticking off each day. Just when it couldn't seem worse, a foolish lunch trip landed me in a military prison. Ten cold, bleak days stretched like ten months. Normal army life suddenly seemed liberating.

My corporate jobs, while less extreme, also constrained freedom. At the telco call centre, shift work granted occasional weekday reprieves from crowded spaces. But subsequent 9-to-5 roles lacked even that. As a business owner, vacationing minds stayed on work. At least there was autonomy—unlike corporate jobs where you must beg for the slightest allowance.

This was something I gleaned from my conversation with Nancy Lai too. Nancy is a former lecturer turned mompreneur who founded an e-commerce business selling maternity wear and play cushions for kids (Lai, 2023). As a working mom, Nancy cherished being able to manage her own calendar and spend more time with her young kids. She gave up the security of employment for freedom over her time.

In an interview, Nancy shared that the motivation to start her business was to gain the flexibility to control her schedule after having her second child. Her corporate job had left her missing out on precious moments due to demanding hours. Nancy was determined not to repeat this experience with her second baby.

So despite giving up a steady teaching income, Nancy took the plunge into entrepreneurship for the autonomy over her time. This allowed her to work from home and be there for her young children during formative years. The case of Nancy illustrates how for some, self-employment offers freedom that trumps even job security.

Beyond just having more time for family, having more time for yourself is already a huge gain that you get as a self-employed person.

You can go hiking, pursue a new hobby and any new activities that intrigue you.

You may think you could probably do it as any employee if you have a WFH policy. That was what a group of Hang Seng Bank management trainees in Hong Kong thought at the start of the COVID-19 pandemic in 2020. They skipped working from home to go hiking, posting photos on Instagram tagged 'best WFH activity'. The bank management was unamused and issued the employees warning letters (Tan, 2023).

With RTO (Return-to-Office) slowly reinstating across companies, you may not even have WFH days anymore to try your luck with. As of this writing, companies like Lark and ANEXT are already on five-days RTO. More should follow.

Self-employment finally returned the freedom lost since childhood. Absolute authority over my calendar and output flips work from being a chore to a choice. Hobbies, family time, and new pursuits fill once wasted hours. No begging superiors for permission or risking warning letters for unauthorized adventures.

The allure of entrepreneurship is strong. The autonomy, purpose, and freedom are intoxicating elixirs. But the security and stability of a corporate job also have magnetic appeal. Making the leap is far from an easy choice.

Yet there comes a point when the soul-sucking negatives of traditional employment outweigh any perks. When your work goes from energizing to demoralizing, a breaking point is nearing. The question that becomes crucial is 'What is holding you back from a more aligned life?'

If you find yourself nodding along to the signs and stories shared, it could be time for reflection. Is the security of the present really worth sacrificing meaning, passion, and well-being in the future? Consider what your eighty-year-old self would tell you to do.

The corporate path of least resistance will always beckon. But deep down, you feel the stirrings of a greater calling. Your time here is fleeting. Instead of sleepwalking through roles misaligned with your gifts, awaken to your higher purpose.

You deserve work that makes you come alive, not merely pays the bills. People who uplift you, not just tolerate you. A bold life lived on your own terms, not confined by convention.

The road ahead requires courage. But waiting only prolongs the inevitable day when you can deny your truth no more. Roam free and write the story you were meant to live. Take the first step today towards the freedom to self-direct your career and build a business driven by your internal compass, not external validation.

This is your one chance to leave your unique stamp on the world. Will you seize it? I hope so, because the world needs more people brave enough to chart their own course and live life their way.

I believe you have that courage within. Let it shine bright. Your gifts are needed.

Key Takeaways

- Reflect deeply on what you value most—freedom, purpose, autonomy? Is your current work aligned?
- Weigh whether the security of employment outweighs daily demoralization.
- Ask yourself 'What is holding me back from more aligned work?' to find clarity.
- Have faith in your latent talents and capacity for growth. You likely underestimate your abilities.

It's natural to feel fear. Courage means moving forward despite uncertainty.

The time is now. You are ready. Make the leap and take charge of your career. Fulfilment awaits on the other side of convention. Your gifts are needed. It's time to share them.

SOLOPRENEUR SPOTLIGHT

From Company Man to Solopreneur: Andy Schmidt's Inspiring Journey to Finding Purpose Through Self-Employment

Like many driven professionals, Andy Schmidt spent decades climbing the corporate ladder without ever questioning the path (Schmidt, 2023). He had secured a coveted role as a financial controller at an MNC by his mid-thirties through hard work and perseverance. To outsiders, Andy was the portrait of success—good pay, respectable title, financial security.

Yet, internally, he couldn't shake the nagging doubt that merely excelling at his job did not equate to a life of meaning. There had to be more to life than dutifully putting in the 9-to-5 each day.

This introspection was sparked after having an illuminating conversation with some former corporate colleagues. Andy asked them frankly: 'What is your biggest regret looking back on your career?' Their resounding response: 'Working too hard chasing titles and not spending enough time with family.'

Hearing the same refrain voiced repeatedly struck Andy as an almost existential warning. He realized he was headed down an identical path of chasing credentials without joy or purpose. It was time for a drastic change.

In 2012, at the height of his corporate success, Andy took the leap into self-employment. He left to intentionalize a life designed with purpose, not just defined by a pay cheque.

It was a plunge into the unknown world beyond the corporate safety net. Financial security was replaced by uncertainty. Business development skills had to be built from scratch. His identity shifted from company man to solopreneur.

Like any entrepreneurial journey, the road was filled with twists and self-doubt. But Andy leveraged the same grit that had fuelled his corporate rise to propel himself forward as a business owner. He learned to embrace uncertainty and stay resilient through failures on the path to eventual success.

Curating Community and Mentors as a Lifeline

Transitioning from an office environment filled with colleagues to working solo was Andy's first major adjustment. He soon realized entrepreneurship could feel extremely isolating without camaraderie.

To fill this gap, Andy's proactively built relationships with fellow solopreneurs blossomed into a valuable support network. Through platforms like LinkedIn, he forged connections that provided essential advice, empathy, and strength during challenging times. These friendships offered a crucial sense of community and shared experience, proving that camaraderie among founders can be a powerful resource.

Andy also stresses the importance of identifying mentors— both within and outside your industry—to provide guidance gleaned from their own journeys. He finds nuggets of wisdom often arise in unexpected places through keeping an open and curious mindset.

While the formal mentor network remained elusive, Andy wasn't one to miss out on unexpected pathways to growth. It was through a casual coffee chat with a LinkedIn connection that he ventured into the realm of mindfulness meditation. Initially intrigued by the concept, he took a leap of faith and joined a 'teaser workshop'. This brief introduction opened the door to a longer, guided training, eventually blossoming into a personal practice that became a game-changer. The simple yet powerful ritual of mindfulness helped him stay focused and enhance his creativity, proving invaluable during tough times.

The Power of Persistence and Patience

As Andy explored business ideas, missteps were inevitable. An early digital health venture—an Anti-Bullying app for schools in Singapore—failed to gain traction despite a year of intense effort.

Rather than clinging to a single, precarious shoot, Andy learned to cultivate a diverse seedbed of potential. He evolved his approach, recognizing that success wasn't about gambling on one big win, but rather patiently planting and nurturing multiple ventures in parallel. This spread the risk, increased his odds of hitting a jackpot, and opened the door to multiple income streams. Progress felt incremental—a constant cycle of testing, iterating, and refining based on market feedback—but the cumulative effect was undeniable. With his hands in several pots, Andy built a sturdier, more resilient foundation for his entrepreneurial journey.

He likens it to having many horses in the race, recognizing most will fail, but staying ready to gallop ahead when one does break through. This perseverance and avoidance of shortcuts led him to eventually find success with his current venture.

Mastering the Art of the Sale

With no sales background, Andy found business development intensely daunting at first. In the corporate world, revenue seemed to just miraculously materialize without any effort from him!

To power through fear of rejection, Andy utilized his financial acumen to run the numbers on what sales activity would be required to reach his targets. This helped take the emotion out of prospecting and make it a numbers game.

He also realized desperation to close deals too quickly often sabotaged the process. Andy learned to take a consultative approach focused on understanding client needs before pitching solutions.

Most importantly, he made sure to celebrate small wins and activities, not just actual sales, to stay motivated through the ups and downs. Incremental progress and relationship building became markers of success.

Discovering the Art of Work-Life Balance

Perhaps the most important mindset shift for Andy was changing his temporal view of work-life balance to one of work-life harmony.

As a solopreneur, work is no longer segregated into neat nine-hour chunks. Andy realized mindfulness has to be applied to integrating work and personal life rather than forcing false barriers.

Practising consistent morning and evening rituals provides structure while allowing flexibility. Having financial savings to cover basic needs reduced pressure during the start-up phase.

Andy became convinced of the magic power of compounding success, which is built brick by brick through daily tasks that form part of his growth system.

Key Takeaways

- **Question assumptions** – Is your current path actually leading you towards your purpose? Don't be afraid to re-evaluate and course-correct.

- **Evolve your strengths** – Leverage past skills while embracing personal growth. See failures as data points to inform new strategies.
- **Build your community** – Isolation stunts progress. Actively nurture supportive relationships and seek out mentors for guidance.
- **Embrace abundance** – Don't get discouraged by closed doors. Stay resilient and open to new opportunities that align with your values.
- **Celebrate the journey** – Building a business is a marathon, not a sprint. Take time to acknowledge small wins and enjoy the process.
- **Different is better** – In a crowded world, standing out matters. Don't just strive to be good, embrace what makes you unique.
- **Mix it up** – Break free from the default 'learn, earn, retire' script. Design your life by blending work and personal aspirations, not squeezing life into work's gaps.

Andy Schmidt's story illustrates that while entrepreneurship requires courage, we all have the capacity to take charge of designing a purpose-driven life. His example shows that incremental steps compound to build momentum. Progress happens through persistence.

Hopefully this account of one man's pursuit of professional fulfilment sparks ideas for your own journey to finding work filled with meaning. What is calling you to live life by design?

Chapter 3

Overcoming Fears and Self-Doubt

'The cave you fear to enter holds the treasure you seek.'
—Joseph Campbell

As I've mentioned in chapter one, my current self-employment journey is technically my sixth rodeo. I started a recruitment firm in 2004, a headhunting biz in 2010, career coaching agency in 2014, a resume optimization platform and an HR consultancy in 2016. That's a lot of entrepreneurial attempts!

With that many crash and burn ventures under my belt, you'd think I'd have nerves of steel by now and could embark on my next entrepreneurial endeavour with eyes closed, using just my pinky fingers to type. Not quite.

While I've accumulated ample street cred thanks to those serial failures, the familiar fears still manage to creep in. Can this new venture actually work or will it be yet another addition to my Chamber of Shame? Will I make enough moolah to afford avocado toasts and $10 lattes at hipster cafes? Or will I be relegated to sipping water sadly flavoured with my own tears while choking down stale instant coffee granules?

And of course, there's the looming fear of being seen as a 'wantrepreneur'—someone who couldn't cut it in the corporate world and pathetically resorted to working for themselves.

But step one (or maybe step zero) before taking the self-employment leap is getting a handle on those fears and slaying those entrepreneurial demons.

Fear Setting

There's this neat exercise called fear setting (Ferriss, 2017), popularized by productivity guru and author Tim Ferriss. It's like next-level worry journaling—you meticulously jot down all the disastrous what-ifs and worst-case scenarios that are holding you back, then figure out actionable plans to prevent or fix each one should it occur.

Tim Ferriss' fear setting is a powerful exercise that helps you overcome your fears and take action on your goals. It is based on an ancient stoic practice called *premeditatio malorum*, which means 'the premeditation of evils'.

The idea is to imagine the worst-case scenarios that could happen if you do something you are afraid of, and then write down how you would prevent them, repair them, or cope with them. You also write down the benefits of taking action and the costs of inaction. By doing this, you can reduce the impact of your fears, increase your confidence, and make better decisions.

Tim Ferris recommends doing fear setting at least once a quarter, or whenever you face a big decision or an opportunity that scares you. He suggests using three pages to do the exercise, following these steps:

- Page 1: *Define* – Write down all the things that could go wrong if you take action. Be specific and realistic. For each item, rate how likely it is to happen on a scale of 0 to 10, where 0 is impossible and 10 is certain.
- Page 2: *Prevent* – Write down what you can do to prevent or decrease the likelihood of each item on page 1 from

happening. For each item, rate how effective your prevention strategy is on a scale of 0 to 10, where 0 is useless and 10 is foolproof.

- Page 3: *Repair* – Write down what you can do to fix or mitigate the damage of each item on page 1 if it happens. For each item, rate how easy your repair strategy is on a scale of 0 to 10, where 0 is impossible and 10 is effortless.
- Bonus Page: *Benefits and Costs* – Write down what are the benefits of taking action, both in the short term and in the long term. Be specific and realistic. Then write down what are the costs of not taking action, both in the short term and in the long term. Be honest and realistic.

After completing the exercise, review your pages and ask yourself these questions:

- What are the most likely and most impactful items on page 1?
- How can I focus on the most effective and easiest items on page 2 and page 3?
- How do the benefits of taking action outweigh the costs of not taking action?

By answering these questions, you can gain clarity and perspective on your situation, and overcome your fears with rational thinking and action planning.

Regret Minimization Framework

Another mind trick that can help in your pivot deliberations is called the Regret Minimization Framework (Ibrahim, 2021). This gem comes courtesy of Amazon's head honcho, Jeff Bezos.

The story behind Jeff Bezos' Regret Minimization Framework is that he used it to make the decision to leave his job and founded

Amazon in 1994. He was working at a hedge fund in New York City, but he had an idea to sell books online.

He approached his boss with the idea, but his boss told him to take forty-eight hours to think about it. Bezos then projected himself forward to age eighty and asked himself what he would regret not doing. He realized that he would regret not trying to participate in the internet boom, even if he failed. He decided that minimizing his regrets later in life was more important than staying in his comfortable job.

He explained his framework in an interview with the Academy of Achievement (Bezos, 2017):

> 'I wanted to project myself forward to age 80 and say, "Okay, now I'm looking back on my life. I want to have minimized the number of regrets I have." I knew that when I was 80 I was not going to regret having tried this. I was not going to regret trying to participate in this thing called the Internet that I thought was going to be a really big deal. I knew that if I failed I wouldn't regret that, but I knew the one thing I might regret is not ever having tried. I knew that that would haunt me every day, and so, when I thought about it that way it was an incredibly easy decision.'

My friend CheeTung also gave this Regret Minimization exercise a go when he was deciding whether to leave his plum strategy consulting position.

As a father of three young girls, the thought of playing it safe in his plum strategy consulting position gnawed at him. He envisioned a future where his daughters grew up in a world he'd only helped advise on, a world shaped by tech he never dared to build. The regret of missing out on this technological revolution, this golden age of innovation, loomed large.

He weighed the comfortable security of his corporate job against the exhilarating, albeit uncertain, path of entrepreneurship.

The potential rewards were immense—the chance to shape the future, to leave a tangible legacy, to learn and grow in ways a corporate cubicle could never offer. Sure, failure was a possibility, but even that held a strange allure. It meant taking a calculated risk, pushing himself beyond his comfort zone, and returning with invaluable skills, networks, and a perspective that would differentiate him forever.

'The worst that can happen is I come back to a corporate job,' he'd reasoned. 'But the potential benefits—the entrepreneurial spirit instilled in my daughters, the skills honed in the crucible of startup life, the connections forged with the pioneers of tomorrow—far outweigh the risks.'

Years later, with his own successful start-up thriving, he knows he made the right call. The regret he once feared has been replaced by a profound sense of accomplishment, a legacy he's building not just for his daughters, but for the future itself. He didn't want to live with the nagging what ifs—no regrets!

What would your eighty-year-old self advise you to do? How can you minimize future remorse and maximize fulfilment? Listen to that inner elderly sage, they usually know best.

Discomfort Is the New Comfort Zone

Let's be real—no career pivot comes with training wheels. It's more like an unpredictable Indiana Jones style adventure into the unknown—thrilling yet terrifying in equal measure. Doubt, uncertainty, stress, and imposter syndrome will likely be your boon companions, especially in the early phases of your transition. It's about leaning into discomfort and repeatedly pushing past your limits until edgy becomes your new normal.

I experienced major discomfort when I first dipped my toe into the solo self-employment pool after years in corporate life. Putting myself out there felt unnatural—I had to push past my introverted tendencies to cold call and email past co-workers, shamelessly begging them to toss any freelance work they could my way.

Those initial uncomfortable conversations made me squeamish. But I forced myself to push through and landed my first client. Then the next cold call got a little easier. The one after that became easier still. Before long, I'd gotten comfortable with the discomfort.

It's like strength training at the gym—your first week leaves you achingly sore, but stick with it and those weights start to feel lighter. Your perseverance muscle gets built. Soon you're ready to incrementally increase the challenge again.

There are many studies that show that persistence correlates to success in various domains of life, such as education (Comings, 2007), work (Wilmot & Ones, 2019), sports (World Athletics, 2020), and personal growth (Pradeepa, 2023). Persistence is the quality of continuing to pursue a goal or passion despite difficulties or obstacles. It is also known as perseverance, grit, determination, or resilience. Persistence is important for success because it:

- Turns people into experts. Persistence allows people to practise and improve their skills over time, which leads to mastery and expertise. Research has shown that deliberate practise, which involves setting specific goals, getting feedback, and focusing on areas of improvement, is essential for achieving high levels of performance in any field (Anna Katharina Schaffner, 2020).
- Motivates people to try harder. Persistence fuels people's passion and drive to achieve their goals. It also helps them overcome challenges and setbacks by making them more optimistic, confident, and resilient. Research has shown that people who are persistent tend to have a growth mindset, which means they believe that their abilities can be developed through effort and learning (Ryan, 2023).

- Shows their ambition. Persistence demonstrates people's commitment and dedication to their goals and passions. It also shows their willingness to take risks, learn from failure, and seek feedback. Research has shown that people who are persistent tend to have higher levels of achievement motivation, which means they have a strong desire to excel and perform well (Burke, 2021).

The same goes for your career pivot fortitude. Be mentally prepared to feel some ouch at first. But remember that ouch is actually the necessary growing pain of progress as you climb towards building a more energizing and aligned work life. With the right mindset, you've so got this! Which leads me to the following:

Cultivate a Growth Mindset

You've probably heard the phrase 'It's all about mindset', and you may have shrugged it off as a trite, oversimplified mantra. But think about it: how many times has your own belief system set the course of your actions? Our attitudes shape our realities, and adopting a growth mindset—the belief that our abilities and intelligence can be developed through dedication, hard work, and the magic of learning—is the first step towards embracing change.

Maintaining positivity during periods of significant change can seem like a daunting task. But with the right techniques, it is possible to cultivate a positive outlook and counter self-limiting beliefs.

Embrace Challenges and Learn from Mistakes

A good way to cultivate a growth mindset is to embrace challenges and learn from mistakes. Instead of avoiding difficult tasks or giving up when faced with obstacles, you can see them as opportunities to grow and improve. By viewing mistakes as feedback, not failure, you can learn from them and avoid repeating them in the future.

One thing that I do to embrace challenges is to set SMART goals for myself. SMART stands for Specific, Measurable, Achievable, Relevant, and Time-bound. These are criteria that help me define and track my progress towards my desired outcomes. For example, instead of saying 'I want to be a better writer,' I would say 'I want to write a 500-word blog post on growth mindset by next Friday.'

If you are like me and tend to find goals overwhelming (and hence procrastinate), you can consider the 'Two-Minute Rule'. James Clear explained this simple strategy in his book *Atomic Habits* (Clear, 2018)—scale down anything you wish to do into a two-minute version. Instead of reading thirty pages, read one page. Instead of folding the laundry, just fold one pair of socks. The notion is to set it up as a gateway habit to bigger things.

Celebrate Small Wins and Appreciate Effort

You can also cultivate a growth mindset by celebrating small wins and appreciating effort. Rather than focusing on the end result or comparing yourself to others, you can acknowledge and celebrate the steps you take towards your goals. By doing so, you can boost your motivation and confidence, and reinforce the positive habits that lead to success.

An easy way to celebrate small wins is to use a habit tracker app, such as Habitica, Streaks, or Done. These apps will help to keep track of the habits that you want to build or break, and reward you with points, badges, or other incentives. For example, if I want to read more books, I would set a habit of reading for thirty minutes every day, and see my streak grow as I stick to it.

Practise Mindfulness

Mindfulness—the practice of focusing your attention on the present moment—is a powerful tool to maintain positivity. By concentrating on the 'here and now', you free yourself from past regrets and future anxieties, creating a space for positive thoughts to flourish.

This is how I typically start my day, a guided meditation of ten to fifteen minutes. There are many apps that comes with a variety of guided meditations, ranging from loving kindness to focusing on your breathing.

You can try out apps such as Insight Timer, Headspace, or Oak.

Harness the Power of Affirmations

Positive affirmations are statements that challenge negative or unhelpful thoughts. Repeating these phrases like 'I am capable of growth', or 'I welcome change with an open mind', can shape your subconscious mind, boosting self-confidence and positivity.

I do this in the form of another app that I learned from Tim Ferriss. The 5 Minute Journal app is a quick and easy way to note down aspects of your day.

It begins with three things you are grateful for, what you hope to achieve, and your daily affirmation.

At a time when I was deep in debt, my daily affirmation was 'We got this, buddy!'

It might seem silly but that was what I came back to draw strength from when things got overwhelming.

Naive Optimism

When contemplating any big career leap into the unknown, it's easy to default to overthinking worst-case doomsday scenarios. What if I go broke? What if I get laughed out of the industry?

What if I have to abandon my life, flee town, and change my name to start over? This kind of obsessive negativity can paralyse you.

I missed out on a multi-million-dollar business opportunity because I overthought and played it safe.

A few years ago, I was one of the early customers of a payroll software start-up. I had kept in touch with the founders, who were impressed by my marketing skills and experience. They offered me a chance to join them as their CMO and partner, and help them scale their business to the next level.

But I let my overthinking get the better of me.

I was not ready to commit fully to their vision, and I wanted to hedge my bets. I asked them to pay me as a consultant first, so I could earn some money regardless of the outcome. I thought I was being smart, but I was actually being short-sighted.

They did not agree to my terms, and the conversation ended there.

Two years later, I found out that they had sold their business to a Japanese buyer for over US$6 million. I was stunned and filled with regret. I contacted the founder who had invited me, and he told me that they could have gotten an even higher valuation if I had joined them. By my own estimate, I could have made $2 million from the deal. I felt like I had thrown away a golden opportunity because of my fear and doubt.

When he approached me again for another venture, I did not hesitate to say yes. I did not want to repeat the same mistake. Unfortunately, that venture did not work out, but I learned a valuable lesson from my experience.

Engineer, inventor, and YouTuber Mark Rober has a more elegant term for this. In his commencement speech at MIT in 2023, he called it 'naive optimism' (Rober, 2023), which is the idea of being optimistic about your future opportunities without being too aware of the challenges and risks ahead.

He said that naive optimism can help you overcome self-doubt and fear of failure, and motivate you to pursue your passions and dreams. His own experiences of applying naive optimism in his engineering projects led him to landing a rover on Mars, building a glitter bomb for package thieves, and creating a squirrel obstacle course.

Here are some possible ways to apply naive optimism in your life:

- Think of how your strengths can bring other good things to your self-employment. For example, if you are good at writing, designing, or coding, think of how you can use these talents to create value for your clients, expand your portfolio, or diversify your income streams. Don't limit yourself to what you already know or do.

- Think of future events that can also happen as a result of your self-employment. For example, if you have a goal of earning a certain amount of money, reaching a certain number of clients, or creating a certain product or service, think of how you will feel when you achieve it, how it will benefit you and others, and what other opportunities it will open up for you. Don't focus on the obstacles or difficulties that might prevent you from reaching your goal.

- Remember, tomorrow is another day. For example, if things don't go as planned in your self-employment, don't give up or lose hope. Learn from your experience and try again. Be resilient and adaptable. Remember that self-employment is not a linear path, but a dynamic and evolving one. You can always change your direction, strategy, or niche if needed.

Writer Lawrence Yeo has an almost similar story when he decided to take the leap from a corporate job to a music career, and how it led to many unexpected and rewarding outcomes (Adney, n.d.).

He argues that taking the leap is not irrational, but rather a rational way of fulfilling one's potential and creating value for the world. Taking the leap is not about abandoning reason, but rather using reason to guide your intuition. He suggests that one can use logic to analyse your current situation and your desired outcome, and then use intuition to bridge the gap between them. He says that 'logic is the map, but intuition is the compass'.

And it isn't about risking everything, but rather managing risk in a smart way. Lawrence advises that one should have a backup plan in case things don't work out, and that you should start small and test your ideas before scaling up. He says that 'taking the leap is not about being reckless but being resourceful'.

Lastly, taking the leap is not about achieving a specific goal, but rather discovering new possibilities. It can open up many doors that you didn't even know existed, and that you should be open to exploring them. According to Lawrence, 'Taking the leap is not about reaching a destination, but embarking on a journey.'

While you don't want to be reckless, a little naive optimism can help calm the nervous mental chatter. Be bold in saying yes, knowing you'll figure out solutions as challenges arise. Progress and results come from action.

Work-Life Balance: The Three Alarm System

Establishing healthy boundaries and managing stress becomes your own responsibility without an organization's structure. The temptation is to work non-stop, but that pace leads to burnout. Sustainable self-employment requires intentional boundaries.

I've tried techniques like Pomodoro and timeboxing, which are both forms of time management that involve breaking down work into fixed intervals. Pomodoro is segments of twenty-five minutes of work followed by five-minute breaks, while timeboxing is setting a specific time limit for any task, regardless of its size or complexity. However, I found that these methods were not enough for me. With my squirrel brain, what I needed was laser focus, the ability to concentrate on one thing without any distractions or interruptions. Laser focus is key to time management because it helps you get more done in less time and with higher quality. Professor Cal Newport's concept of 'deep work' resonates—the ability to concentrate without distraction on cognitively demanding tasks (Newport, *Deep Work: Rules for Focused Success in a Distracted World*, 2016).

Newport argues deep work fuels productivity and meaning. But it's rare in today's distraction-laden environment. Multitasking frazzles the brain, diminishing work quality, increasing stress, and reducing satisfaction.

To reclaim deep work, Newport advises scheduling uninterrupted blocks for focused efforts, setting specific goals for each block, and reviewing afterwards to celebrate wins and improve.

The principles transformed my output. But concentration still takes effort. An idea from coach Eric Partaker helped optimize my focus. His 'Three Alarms' sets a daily alarm for your 'best self' in health, work, and home (Partaker, 2020). The identity prompt shapes your actions.

My Apple Watch alerts me to do chin-ups, single-task intensely, and be a present father. The technique aligns my behaviour to my values in each realm. Dedicating focused energy avoids neglecting one priority for another.

With simple techniques, we can structure self-employment to energize, not deplete us. The path requires diligence, but conscious choices transform work from being a draining chore to a vitalizing calling.

But establishing boundaries is an art that requires experimentation. It's about learning what works for you, not blindly following someone else's system. For example,

I initially tried rigid timeboxing but found it too constraining. I've learned to go with the flow once I'm in a state of deep focus, rather than watching the clock.

On the other hand, I need structure for starting my day intentionally rather than reactively. The Three Alarms technique has been invaluable to orient myself before heading into work mode. Similarly, having set end times and family rituals provide closure and transition from work time.

As we discussed earlier, cultivating a growth mindset is the first step towards embracing change and maintaining positivity. But that's not enough. Besides techniques, cultivating the right mindset is key to managing our energy. Seeing self-employment as an exhilarating challenge rather than a burden reduces its toll. When we attach meaning to our work, it uplifts rather than drains us. Passion fuels resilience.

And while passion comes from within, community can also empower us to avoid isolation and burnout as solo entrepreneurs. Having a supportive circle of fellow solopreneurs helps normalize the ups and downs of self-employment. They can relate to your unique struggles in a way your corporate friends can't.

For example, I'm part of a small private mastermind group that meets monthly to share knowledge and provide mutual encouragement. We've become each other's informal advisers and accountability partners. It gives me both inspiration and reprieve.

Building community allows us to replenish our wells so we can sustainably give our gifts to clients. At the end of day, maintaining a self-care routine and work-life balance is about listening inward. It's the journey, not the destination. With self-compassion, we can rewrite the rules to thrive in our own way.

Overcoming Fear and Self-Doubt

The incredible Anne Sullivan didn't initially feel qualified teaching the remarkable Helen Keller (Joseph P.Lash, 1997).

Despite being twenty years old with minimal formal education, Anne accepted the immense challenge of educating a child both blind and deaf.

Anne herself had lost her sight when she was five, so she understood Helen's isolation in the dark, silent world. But she still doubted her capacity to meet the needs of a student who struggled with severe communication barriers and temper outbursts.

However, Anne persisted through self-doubt and found creative ways to connect with Helen. She learned finger spelling and signed letters into Helen's palm so she could feel words tactilely. This breakthrough unlocked language for Helen, allowing her an outlet to express her frustrations.

With compassion and patience, Anne empowered Helen to blossom. Helen eventually learned to speak, write, attend college, and became an iconic author and activist. Anne's mentorship enabled one of the most remarkable transformations in history.

Anne Sullivan's story demonstrates that ability is not fixed. Qualifications on paper may impress, but grit and willingness to learn can enable success beyond formal credentials. Like Anne, have faith in your latent potential. Growth comes more from perseverance than pedigree.

So how do you work through all the worries and butterflies that go along with career pivoting? Here are some proven strategies along with examples from my own journey:

1. Visualize yourself succeeding. Picture yourself landing clients, growing your business, and achieving your goals. Envisioning success can help drive it. I still get nervous before every client pitch, so I spend time beforehand picturing them saying yes.

2. Focus on progress, not perfection. Don't expect to quickly master every aspect of solo work. Celebrate small wins and milestones. Progress is non-linear. When I first started consulting, I was thrilled just to land one

client. That gave me hope I could eventually build a whole business.

3. Separate thoughts from facts. Just because you think something negative will happen doesn't mean it's true. Stick to the facts. My inner pessimist constantly imagines worst-case scenarios that never end up happening. I have to remind myself of what's factual.

4. Break big goals into smaller steps. Trying to eat the whole elephant in one bite is daunting. Take it step-by-step. With my coaching business, we started by identifying our first ten prospective clients to reach out to. Not overwhelming.

5. Spend time with supportive people. Surround yourself with those who believe in you, especially during times of doubt. My wife was my rock when I struggled with imposter syndrome in my early consulting days. Her faith kept me going.

6. Be kind to yourself. Don't beat yourself up for having doubts or struggling sometimes. Self-compassion bolsters resilience. I used to feel like a failure for not mastering self-employment overnight. Now I know growing takes time.

The uncertainty of career change ignites universal fears—'What if I fail?' 'What if I can't pay the bills?' 'Who am I without my job title?' You are not alone in these doubts. Even the most confident hide secret insecurities.

But your business does not require bravado or brazenness. Real courage is being scared but taking the next step anyway. Heroes feel the same fear as everyone else, they just refuse to surrender to it.

When uncertainty strikes, avoid fixating on perfect plans. As serial entrepreneur and LinkedIn co-founder Reid Hoffman famously said, 'You jump off the cliff and assemble an airplane on the way down' (Baer, 2013). Progress begins with saying yes before you feel ready. The rest you can figure out.

Your path forward will meander, not follow a straight line. Setbacks assure you are heading somewhere interesting. Each twist holds lessons to pave smoother trails.

As Part I of the book comes to a close, you now have tools to quiet limiting voices and focus on possibilities:

- Harness optimism – believe you will navigate obstacles creatively.
- Reframe setbacks – they prepare you for future success.
- Visualize desired outcomes – imagine how achieving your goals will feel.
- Limit comparisons – focus on your authentic definition of success.
- Celebrate small wins – progress fuels motivation.

At times the road may seem lonely. But others walk with you in spirit, cheering you onwards. The world needs more people brave enough to live life their own way. Your gifts are needed.

Dig deep and trust your vision. Let passion drown out fear. With consistent action, you will look back one day amazed at how far you've come. Your future self is cheering for you.

The time is now. Tune out the noise and take the first step. The freedom to build a life and work aligned with what makes you come alive awaits. This is your one wild and precious life. Seize it courageously!

Key Takeaways

- Fear setting and regret minimization are two complementary frameworks to help you overcome your fears and make better decisions. By defining the worst-case scenarios and the potential regrets, you can plan ahead and take action accordingly.

- Embracing discomfort and cultivating a growth mindset are two essential skills to help you grow and learn from challenges. By pushing your boundaries and celebrating your efforts, you can develop confidence and resilience.

- Naive optimism and visualization are two powerful techniques to help you focus on the positive and the possible. By imagining the best outcomes and the steps to achieve them, you can overcome doubts and obstacles.

- Eric Partaker's daily Three Alarms and community support are two practical ways to help you balance your work and life. By setting reminders for your health, work, and personal goals, and by finding an accountability group, you can stay motivated and productive.

- Self-compassion is the key to help you manage your fears and doubts. By being kind to yourself and acknowledging your feelings, you can cope with stress and anxiety.

Part II

Launching Your Self-Employment Venture

Chapter 4

Discovering Your Business Idea

'Don't worry about failure; you only have to be right once.'
—Drew Houston

You're fired up, mentally ready to pivot to self-employment. But with limitless possibilities before you, indecision can take hold. Researchers call this 'analysis paralysis'.

Psychologists like William Edmun Hick and Ray Hyman researched this decision fatigue. Hick's Law shows that more choices increase deliberation time logarithmically (Hick, 1952). This explains why we stare blankly at a 200-item Hong Kong café menu and it overwhelms our ability to decide.

When pivoting careers, avoid overthinking yourself into inertia. The key is narrowing your focus. As Steve Jobs advised Stanford graduates, 'Don't let the noise of others' opinions drown out your own inner voice.' (Stanford, 2008)

To find clarity amid the clamour of options, start by looking inward. Tune out external voices to hear your inner wisdom. Reflect on past experiences that brought joy or frustration. Pay attention to what energizes you. Then complement self-exploration by seeking outside perspectives from those who know you well.

By balancing internal and external insights, you gain self-knowledge to make choices aligned with your strengths. The path forward emerges one step at a time.

Self-Reflection

An easy first step to narrowing your focus is identify what you hate doing. Our dislikes reveal true preferences and illuminate potential paths.

For instance, I realized teaching wasn't for me when frustrations mounted after teaching digital marketing and entrepreneurship. No matter the helpful students, one dismissive participant could infuriate me. Other instructors took criticism in stride, but I lacked their unflappable temperament. After multiple sleepless nights, I stopped teaching.

This experience highlighted that my strengths lay elsewhere. While unpleasant, it provided clarity. As pioneering inventor Buckminster Fuller put it, 'There is only one real failure in life that is possible, and that is not to be true to the best one knows.' (Fuller, 1970)

Assessment Spotlight

Self-reflection has limits. We often notice others' talents before our own. Complement inner wisdom with outside perspectives.

Sometimes, it can be hard to figure out what you really enjoy or dislike doing. That's why assessment tools can be useful. They can help you discover more about yourself, your personality, your motivations, and your preferences. By taking different assessments and comparing the results, you can find patterns and insights that can guide your career choices.

Here are some examples of assessment tools that can help you identify what you dislike:

1. **Birkman Method Assessment:**[1] This is a comprehensive personality and motivational assessment that includes questions to help uncover occupations and activities you would dislike. It identifies stress behaviours and needs to determine your ideal work environment.

2. **Truity's Typefinder:**[2] This assessment uses questions based on the Myers-Briggs personality framework to identify your likely personality type. Knowing your type can help reveal jobs and roles you may dislike based on your natural preferences.

Don't rely on any single assessment, though. Look for the common threads across multiple tools. Look for overlap between inner and outer perspectives. Patterns emerge about your strengths, values, and ideal work environment.

Keep in mind even the best instruments have flaws. Use assessments thoughtfully to spur meaningful self-reflection, not as an absolute answer. When inner and outer wisdom align, you gain confidence to take the next step.

Identifying Your Superpowers

After pinpointing your dislikes, next is to uncover your superpowers. Identifying your innate strengths requires a multifaceted approach. Depending on any single test or perspective is risky and limited.

One way to uncover your superpowers is to use empirical assessment tools. These are tests that are based on scientific research and data and can help you measure your strengths in various domains. By taking these tests, you can discover aspects

---

[1] https://birkman.com/the-birkman-method

[2] https://www.truity.com/test/type-finder-personality-test-new

of yourself that you may not be aware of, or that you may take for granted. You can also learn how to leverage your strengths in different situations and contexts.

For example, you can try the free Red Bull Wingfinder test (Red Bull, n.d.).[3]

Developed by psychologists, it measures strengths across four key areas:

- Connections – evaluating communication style, relationship-building skills, emotional intelligence
- Thinking – assessing information processing, strategic planning, decision-making
- Creativity – measuring idea generation, innovation, problem-solving ability
- Drive – gauging resilience, self-motivation, achievement drive

After taking Wingfinder's in-depth assessment myself, many previously unknown strengths emerged. For instance, it revealed I have exceptionally high social intelligence and rapport-building skills. This was surprising yet validating, as it explained why colleagues often raved about how comforting and easy it was to talk to me, even about sensitive topics. I've had multiple people open up to me about very personal issues soon after meeting them. The Wingfinder results helped me recognize this empathic communication style is one of my superpowers.

Another excellent self-assessment option is the CliftonStrengths assessment (Gallup, n.d.). This identifies thirty-four potential talent themes and reveals your top five most dominant ones. It provides detailed insights on how to maximize each of your core strengths in different situations. The thirty-minute online test requires quickly responding to 177 descriptive statements. Afterwards, you receive a personalized twenty-page report illuminating your top five themes and how they manifest in your behaviours, attitudes, and abilities.

---

[3] https://www.redbull.com/int-en/wingfinder

GALLUP®   StrengthsFinder®

Your Signature Themes

SURVEY COMPLETION DATE: 09-28-2015

Adrian Tan

Many years of research conducted by The Gallup Organization suggest that the most effective people are those who understand their strengths and behaviors. These people are best able to develop strategies to meet and exceed the demands of their daily lives, their careers, and their families.

A review of the knowledge and skills you have acquired can provide a basic sense of your abilities, but an awareness and understanding of your natural talents will provide true insight into the core reasons behind your consistent successes.

Your Signature Themes report presents your five most dominant themes of talent, in the rank order revealed by your responses to StrengthsFinder. Of the 34 themes measured, these are your "top five."

Your Signature Themes are very important in maximizing the talents that lead to your successes. By focusing on your Signature Themes, separately and in combination, you can identify your talents, build them into strengths, and enjoy personal and career success through consistent, near-perfect performance.

Restorative

You love to solve problems. Whereas some are dismayed when they encounter yet another breakdown, you can be energized by it. You enjoy the challenge of analyzing the symptoms, identifying what is wrong, and finding the solution. You may prefer practical problems or conceptual ones or personal ones. You may seek out specific kinds of problems that you have met many times before and that you are confident you can fix. Or you may feel the greatest push when faced with complex and unfamiliar problems. Your exact preferences are determined by your other themes and experiences. But what is certain is that you enjoy bringing things back to life. It is a wonderful feeling to identify the undermining factor(s), eradicate them, and restore something to its true glory. Intuitively, you know that without your intervention, this thing—this machine, this technique, this person, this company—might have ceased to function. You fixed it, resuscitated it, rekindled its vitality. Phrasing it the way you might, you saved it.

Harmony

You look for areas of agreement. In your view there is little to be gained from conflict and friction, so you seek to hold them to a minimum. When you know that the people around you hold differing views, you try to find the common ground. You try to steer them away from confrontation and toward harmony. In fact, harmony is one of your guiding values. You can't quite believe how much time is wasted by people trying to impose their views on others. Wouldn't we all be more productive if we

765177708 (Adrian Tan)   1
© 2000, 2006-2012 Gallup, Inc. All rights reserved.

GALLUP®   StrengthsFinder®

Taking the CliftonStrengths assessment was an eye-opening experience for me. It confirmed strengths I had personally noticed before, like strategic thinking and creative problem-solving. But it also uncovered some powerful talents I hadn't previously identified, such as exceptional discipline, achievement orientation, and activator abilities. Seeing discipline emerge as one of my top themes made sense upon reflection, as I thought back on the relentless drive, organization, and work ethic underpinning much of my career achievements and productivity.

Overall, the combination of Wingfinder and CliftonStrengths tests provided tremendous value by validating strengths I had recognized in myself, while also revealing hidden gems I had been unaware of. They enabled me to appreciate that some of my natural talents are rarer and more powerful than I had realized.

However, self-assessments alone have limits. As mentioned previously, we often notice others' talents more readily than our own. Close friends and colleagues see us in a more objective light, observing skills we exhibit but don't give ourselves enough credit for. Their outside perspective can shine light on latent strengths we have overlooked or taken for granted.

For instance, various managers and colleagues over the years suggested I consider exploring DJing or podcasting long before I ever recognized those abilities in myself. Similarly, they consistently identified strong writing and marketing skills that I had always downplayed in my mind as things anyone could pick up. But their external vantage point helped me recognize those came naturally to me more than most.

As renowned author Cal Newport writes in his book *So Good They Can't Ignore You*, passion often stems from cultivating rare and valuable skills, not the other way around (Newport, *So Good They Can't Ignore You*, 2016). We are likely to become passionate about activities that allow us to exercise our innate strengths and talents. So it's important to pay attention to what energizes you, as well as what trusted others admire or rely on you for. Their observations provide clues about your distinctive superpowers that you may be blind to.

By taking a balanced approach using both internal self-reflection and external feedback, you gain a more accurate and holistic view of your abilities. What you and others recognize as your natural strengths provides important hints about promising work avenues worth exploring next. The path forward comes into focus step-by-step through developing well-rounded self-awareness.

Turning Strengths into Offerings

Pinpointing your superpowers allows tailoring your offerings around them, whether products or services.

A product is a tangible item a customer purchases and owns—a book, car, phone, etc. A service is an intangible activity a customer pays for and experiences, like a haircut, massage, or cab ride.

Some key differences:

- Tangibility – Products can be touched and perceived physically. Services are invisible, though some products are intangible too like software.
- Perishability – Products expire and deteriorate over time. Services are consumed at delivery with no shelf life, though some services can become outdated such as warranty services.
- Quality – Product quality is consistent across units and measurable at purchase. Service quality varies based on provider, customer, and context. It's subjective and hard to measure.
- Ownership – Customers own products to use at will. With services, customers don't own anything, only the experience.
- Production and consumption – Products are produced then consumed later. They can be stored and transported. Services are produced and consumed simultaneously. They can't be inventoried or transported.

Some potential products you could offer:

- *Online courses*: Share your expertise via Udemy, Teachable, or Skillshare. Online courses generate passive income and establish authority. I created a LinkedIn scaling course which continues earning royalties years later (Tan, n.d.).
- *E-books*: Publish e-books showcasing insights and expertise. E-books also work as lead magnets for email list growth to promote other offerings. E-books have low production costs but make great freebies or low-priced products. Media entrepreneur and LinkedIn Top Voice Juliana Chan came up with an e-book about LinkedIn Success Mindset (Chan, n.d.).
- *Physical books*: Share your stories, ideas, and knowledge while building credibility. Books market your other products and services. My first book was with Candid Publishing, which got it into major bookstores (Pang, 2013). That media exposure led to career consulting opportunities.
- *Podcasts*: You can create and host podcasts on topics that interest you and your audience, such as entrepreneurship, lifestyle, culture, or entertainment. Podcasts can help you build a loyal fan base and increase your brand awareness. You can monetize your podcasts by selling sponsorships, ads, merchandise, or premium content. Reginald Koh (better known as Reggie) started *The Financial Coconut* in 2019 (The Financial Coconut, n.d.). They are Singapore's first financial literacy podcast and can commonly be found on top podcast charts on Spotify. He monetizes through ad rolls, and helping companies with their podcast productions.
- *YouTube videos*: You can create and upload videos on YouTube on topics that you are passionate and knowledgeable about, such as travel, fitness, music, or comedy. YouTube videos can help you reach a large and

diverse audience and showcase your personality and creativity. You can monetize your videos by enabling ads, joining the YouTube Partner Program, selling merchandise, or getting sponsorships. Kelvin Tan started his YouTube channel Kelvin Learns Investing[4] on the side in 2006 and has since became a full-time YouTuber talking about money-related stuffs like investing, credit cards, and how to save money to retire early. His channel had 98.9K subscribers and 11 million views as of September 2023.

- *Software*: Meet specific needs through web, mobile, or desktop applications. Charge one-time or recurring fees. Offer free trials, freemium versions, or referral programmes to attract and retain customers. One of my earlier projects was a resume optimization site charging a monthly recurring fee. But software takes significant technical skills and ongoing maintenance. Jon Yongfook Cockle has far better success in this space. He started Bannerbear in 2020 after this previous corporate job at Aviva as their Head of Digital Project & Design. Bannerbear has gone on to $600,000 ARR (annual recurring revenue) as of September 2023 (Yongfook, n.d.).

These products have high barriers to entry. Writing books or developing software takes time regardless of talent levels. Podcasting and YouTube also require honing production skills.

This doesn't mean you shouldn't create them. The payoff from conquering those hurdles is less competition. But as a pragmatist, you likely want some quick wins. That's where services come in.

Services require no elaborate production process. You can offer them immediately by drawing on your strengths and experience.

---

[4] https://www.youtube.com/c/kelvinlearnsinvesting

Some examples:

- *Consulting*: Offer your expertise to help organizations or individuals achieve goals and improve performance. Charge hourly, project-based, or value-based. Consulting leverages your know-how so it's a default option for many mid-career professionals. But you need outstanding people skills and confidence. Eric Tan is one such consultant. Via his company, The Resource Group, he provides consultancy services to Singapore-based companies looking to scale in productivity or to venture into overseas market.

- *Freelancing*: Provide work to clients on a project basis across areas like writing, design, development, photography, or video production. Freelancing enables a flexible schedule and rates. Use platforms like Upwork, Fiverr, or Freelancer to find clients. This can easily build up your portfolio.

- *Fractional Work*: Perform project or part-time work combining multiple roles versus one full-time job. Fractional workers operate like part-time employees, contributing fixed hours and gaining company insights through regular team interactions. Fractional work is the bulk of my work now as I spend twenty hours a week acting as the Fractional Head of Marketing for an enterprise people analytics software company that is expanding into APAC.

- *Coaching*: Help individuals or groups achieve goals around personal growth, career development, performance improvement, leadership, and more. Charge per hour, session, or package. Formats include life coaching, executive coaching, performance coaching, leadership coaching, and beyond. But unlike consultants who offer pre-defined solutions, coaches empower clients to unlock their own potential and chart their own path to success.

Pivoting from training, Steven Lock went into coaching focusing on C-suites and senior management. (More of his story later.)

- *Teaching*: Share your knowledge and passion with students wanting to learn a new skill or topic. Teach via tutoring, mentoring, online courses, workshops, or webinars. Schools often hire adjunct instructors on contract to teach specific needs. Over and above her leadership coaching business, my interview subject Adeline Tiah is also an adjunct lecturer with Singapore University of Social Science lecturing at the School of Business.

You are not restricted by only one option. It could be a combination as long as you have the bandwidth to follow through.

For example, media entrepreneur Juliana Chan not only runs a boutique media company but she also created an online course, e-book, podcast, as well as helps other professionals in growing their LinkedIn.

And that is one of the many beauties of self-employment as you can pick and choose from the buffet table what you like to do and the channel to conduct them from.

My current slate now includes:

- Fractional Head of Marketing for an enterprise that's a people analytics software company
- Content Strategist for SAP SuccessFactors implementation partner
- Digital Marketing Director for a local marketing agency
- Podcast co-host for *Work It* by CNA
- Ad hoc writing, speaking engagements, presentations, marketing promotions
- Sponsorships and ads on my website, podcast, LinkedIn, and YouTube
- My LinkedIn Learning course

And I'm working to monetize my YouTube channel while writing this book you're reading!

It's a dynamic mix based on my superpowers and market appetite. The key is staying agile, testing ideas quickly, and doubling down on what gains traction.

Don't be disheartened if some of them did not work out or just did not appeal to you. It is all part of the discovery process.

As I mentioned before, only after I tried did I realize that I truly do not enjoy teaching and have since ruled out all teaching and training assignments.

To find out your true north star, sometimes you have to make a few wrong turns.

The Power of Specialized Positioning

With a universe of possibilities comes equally fierce competition. In a sea of generalists, avoid becoming just another jack-of-all-trades. When anyone can claim to do everything, differentiation becomes impossible and you race to the bottom on price alone.

Instead, niche down to stand out. Think micro, not macro. Forget casting a wide net hoping to capture every fish. It takes focus to spear one profitable mackerel.

For example, a former CFO could generically offer part-time 'CFO Services'. But specializing as a Fractional CFO for Pre-IPO Fintech Start-ups is a much more targeted niche. This immediately communicates specialized expertise and positioning.

When first building niche credibility, consistent content creation establishes thought leadership. Share unique insights and best practices related to your specialty through articles, blogs, videos, podcasts, and more.

By laser-focusing your positioning instead of remaining a generic jack-of-all-trades, you transform from interchangeable to indispensable in the minds of prospective clients.

Specialization coupled with consistency earns you premium clients at commanding rates.

Rather than diluting your efforts widely, double down on your zone of genius. Meet the market's needs by positioning yourself as a niche solution. Align your skills, knowledge, passion, and offerings into a tight niche target.

When your positioning, passion, and profits all intersect within a clarified niche, work stops feeling like work. You have unlocked the code to getting paid for your specialized superpowers.

So niche down strategically. Forget being an acceptable substitute. Become the preferred specialist in your category so ideal clients seek you out for solutions specifically. The power of an optimized niche makes standing out simple.

The Rise of Fractional Work Arrangements

Fractional work involves taking on professional roles and responsibilities on a part-time, interim basis. Unlike one-off freelance gigs, fractional arrangements tend to be more integrated and long-term, while still retaining flexibility (Multiple, n.d.).

For example, a fractional executive operates similar to a normal full-time employee in terms of job scope, influence, and representation of the company. They participate in leadership team meetings, weigh in on strategic decisions, manage teams or projects cross-functionally, and serve as an empowered representative of the organization.

However, unlike traditional executives, they perform this high-level work on a part-time schedule, typically around twenty hours per week. This allows the company to access seasoned executive-level strategic capabilities, experience, and critical thinking without the inflated expense of a full-time salary, benefits, office space, and other associated costs.

Fractional work is trending for several reasons:

- Cost-effective: Fractional leaders provide executive expertise without the expense of a full-time executive salary and benefits. This works well for budget-conscious or early-stage companies unsure of market appetite.
- Strategic implementation: Fractional leaders possess specialized experience implementing proven best practices, processes, and strategies from past contexts. I get approached because clients value my specific domain expertise.
- Immediate results: Fractional leaders bring fresh eyes, objectivity, and urgency to drive short-term goals and objectives.

While the fractional model first emerged primarily for C-suite roles like CMO, CTO, CIO, CFO, and more, it has expanded successfully to other functions including:

- Fractional Marketing Director
- Fractional Sales Manager
- Fractional Operations Leader
- Fractional Human Resources Business Partner
- Fractional Learning and Development Consultant

Additionally, fractional arrangements are no longer limited to the executive tier. Other professionals across levels are also increasingly working fractionally, including:

- Fractional Account Managers
- Fractional Financial Analysts
- Fractional Graphic Designers
- Fractional Recruiters
- Fractional Social Media Managers

The popularity of fractional work continues to grow as both employers and talent recognize the mutual benefits and flexibility it offers. By combining the strategic impact of specialized experts with customizable scheduling, fractional arrangements provide an agile workforce solution tailored to modern business needs.

For example, Tamanna Bavishi was a full-time Quora Community Manager. But her role shifted when Quora deprioritized community growth.

She evaluated options and chose a fractional community role with Fractionals United, also serving two other companies fractionally. As I am part of the community, she shared her story with me over a Zoom call. Her Quora lay-off taught her multiple income streams are safer than one full-time job. If one client ends the engagement, two others remain.

My fractional scope covers marketing. I spent over a year as Fractional CMO for an HR membership organization at eight hours per week. My current role with the enterprise HR Tech vendor is twenty hours per week with expectations adjusted accordingly.

The key is positioning your niche expertise as compelling value worthy of premium rates. Specialization builds a personal brand that attracts premium clients. Coupling niche skills with fractional flexibility and seniority signals top-tier talent worth retaining long-term.

For instance, a fractional social media manager could focus specifically on fintech clients. This showcases marketing abilities, fractional work advantages, and relevant industry experience.

As another example, an instructional designer with e-learning experience might position themselves as a fractional learning experience consultant specialized in the healthcare sector. This communicates niche expertise that is both flexible and strategic.

In essence, fractional work multiplies the positioning power of your niche. You combine the credibility of specialization with the appeal of a seasoned veteran willing to provide part-time leadership. This fusion offers immense value to clients that boosts your leverage and income-earning potential.

The world is your oyster when you intersect fractional flexibility with a clarified niche. Roles once relegated to rigid full-time employment open up to blended customization. You chart your own course according to strengths rather than traditional norms.

By lining up your superpowers, interests, and availability into a fractional niche combo, you transcend outdated models to create work that works.

Find Your Calling

The search for your ideal business idea can feel like finding a needle in a haystack. With limitless possibilities before you, where do you start?

Begin by looking inward to uncover your innate strengths and interests. Complement self-reflection by seeking insightful external perspectives from those who know you well.

By taking a balanced approach to gain self-awareness, you illuminate promising paths aligned with your talents. Experimentation reveals how you can best add value. Ideas sprout by intersecting your skills with market needs.

Of course, refining your niche and offerings takes trial and error. Not every seed sprouts on first planting. But with patience and dedication, clarity emerges.

Remember that passion often arises from developing rare and valuable expertise. Explore avenues that allow you to exercise skills you excel at.

While nosier roads beckon, maintain focus to become uniquely indispensable. Depth beats breadth when standing out in a crowded market.

The journey requires stamina, but each step unveils more of your distinctive promise. With consistency, your efforts compound as progress builds momentum.

Stay confident that your purpose lies buried within, ready to be uncovered and shared. It's already there—you just have to chip away the excess until its unique form emerges.

Keep the end goal in mind, but celebrate small signs of direction. The path comes into focus one milestone at a time.

Your talents only need the right opportunity to blossom and brighten the world. Believe in your potential and listen to your inner wisdom. The seeds you plant today determine the fruits you harvest tomorrow.

Nurture your gifts patiently and they will mature in time, bearing the sweet nectar of work you love. You've got this!

Key Takeaways

- Decision paralysis and dislikes are two factors that can hinder your career exploration and satisfaction. By reflecting on your preferences and using assessment tools, you can narrow down your options and avoid getting stuck.
- Hidden and transferable strengths are two assets that can help you create value and income from your skills. By using validated assessments and external feedback, you can discover your strengths and apply them to various offerings.
- Niche and fractional are two strategies that can help you stand out and attract clients in a competitive

market. By specializing in a specific area and offering part-time services, you can differentiate yourself and deliver impact.

- Products and services are two types of offerings that you can create based on your skills and goals. Products require more upfront work and investment but can generate passive income. Services can be started quickly and can provide immediate feedback.

Experimentation is the key to finding your ideal career path and offering. By testing your ideas, refining your approach, and focusing on your passions, you can find what works best for you and your clients.

How Motherhood Propelled Nancy Lai to Become a Mumpreneur

As a new mom of two young kids, Nancy Lai struggled to balance corporate work with breastfeeding.

After giving birth to her second child, Nancy looked forward to bonding with the new baby during her maternity leave. But she couldn't have predicted a global pandemic would extend her leave at home by months.

When the COVID-19 circuit breaker suddenly hit, Nancy's maternity leave became a seven-month immersion with her newborn. Long days together while the world stood still allowed deep mother-child bonding.

Now, the thought of leaving her son filled Nancy with anxiety. The pandemic had unexpectedly shifted her priorities entirely.

While Nancy had planned to return to work, she realized she couldn't bear to part from her baby to resume corporate life. The office suddenly seemed like an alien world compared to the new bliss with her boy.

That's when a lightbulb switched on—Nancy had business ideas circulating for years. Why not finally pursue them now? She decided to take the leap into mompreneurship, hoping to shape a flexible career where she could still be a hands-on mum.

Launching Her Ventures as a Lean Start-Up

Nancy established not just one but two start-ups catering to moms and babies—a novel multi-functional breastfeeding clothing line, and foam play furniture for kids.

Having experienced first-hand the pains of breastfeeding and pumping as a working mom, she knew her garment solved a real need. For the foam furniture line, the idea was sparked by wanting to create a safer play environment for her daughter prone to injurious nosebleeds.

In launching both ventures, Nancy applied lessons learned from an unsuccessful tech start-up attempt back in university. This time, she took a lean approach focused on testing demand before over-investing.

She launched new products in small test batches, refined them based on user feedback, then manufactured more colours and variants only after validating product-market fit. This nimble and scrappy go-to-market strategy allowed her to bootstrap the ventures without external funding.

Tapping Organic Marketing Tactics

As a solopreneur, Nancy had to get creative on the marketing front with limited time and resources. She found social media ads and Google search ads delivered better returns than influencer promotions.

Pop-up play events allowed hands-on product demos resulting in high conversion rates. Partnerships with complementary brands expanded her reach. But Nancy credits old-fashioned word-of-mouth as most powerful, with referrals among mom groups providing continuous sales.

Maintaining Work-Life Integration

Beyond getting the business fundamentals right, Nancy focuses on maintaining work-life integration as a solopreneur. She blocks mornings for core business hours based on her childcare schedule. Her calendar ensures focused time for both work and family.

While Nancy feels the isolation of working alone at times, she stays motivated by keeping costs low and making gradual progress. Having financial buffers in place and cutting discretionary spending reduced pressure during the start-up phase.

Most of all, Nancy checks in frequently on her reason for starting this journey—to create flexibility allowing precious time with her young kids. Their smiles re-energize her commitment.

Key Takeaways from Nancy's Experience

- Validate product ideas quickly and cheaply before over-investing. Iteratively refine based on user feedback.
- Bootstrap your start-up creatively through lean marketing tactics with minimal budget.
- Build organic community and word-of-mouth through exceptional products and customer experience.
- Maintain work-life integration disciplines, not just superficial work-life balance.
- Anchor yourself in your core motivation and purpose during difficult stretches.

Nancy Lai's story illustrates how solopreneurship can unlock work-life flexibility without sacrificing professional success. With grit, resourcefulness, and maintaining perspective, she continues to nurture her homegrown start-ups while blending entrepreneurship with purposeful parenting.

Chapter 5

Doing the Math: Crunching the Numbers

'Watch the costs and the profits will take care of themselves.'
—Andrew Carnegie

The crimson notice from my bank seemed to mock me. Its arrival wasn't a surprise; the pile of similar reminders was testament to that. It was another missed loan payment, another financial storm I already knew was brewing.

Leaving my recruitment business in 2015 had been a gamble. Overnight, my $13,000 monthly income plummeted to a meagre $2,000 as I embraced a new path as a private career coach. While my co-authored career guidebook brought in some business, it was a mere drop in the bucket compared to the inflated expenses I'd inherited from my previous life.

Though the exit deal offered some financial cushion, most of it went straight to plugging the gaping holes left by years of debt. Financial management had never been my strong suit and it took me a few years of hard knocks to learn the lessons well.

Financial Runway

Remember CheeTung from chapter three? Avoiding future regrets was his key reason to quit his high-paying corporate job and start an HR Tech on employee engagement.

He also made sure he fulfilled another pre-requisite before going all in. And that is he had eighteen months of financial runway.

This runway was sufficient to sustain him and his family for the next eighteen months even if he wasn't drawing a salary from his new venture.

Mumpreneur Nancy Lai of A Mighty Venture shared with me a similar story (Lai, 2023). She made sure she had at least five years of mortgage repayment before she decided to kick-start her maternity wear and kids play mattresses business.

Financial runway is crucial when pivoting from a career to self-employment for several important reasons:

- Revenue Lag Time: When starting a new business, there is often a gap between the initial investment and generating enough revenue to cover costs and turn a profit. Savings provide a runway to operate while ramping up sales.
- Inconsistent Early Income: Income tends to be inconsistent and unpredictable in the early stages of self-employment. Existing savings help smooth out dips in revenue before income steadies.
- Capital Investment: Starting a business requires significant upfront capital to cover expenses like licenses, equipment, and marketing before sales pick up. Savings provides this needed capital.
- Proof of Concept: A longer financial runway allows the time needed to refine concepts, product/market fit and demonstrate proof of concept before profitability.
- Personal Financial Needs: Regular pay cheques from employment often fund living expenses. Savings provides a bridge to cover personal costs during the business growth phase.
- Emergency Buffer: Unexpected emergencies, costs, or delays could quickly sink a new business without cash reserves to absorb the hit.

This is what drove Phil Knight, co-founder of Nike, to continue working as an accountant for several years while slowly building his side business, Blue Ribbon Sports, which was later renamed Nike (Knight, 2016).

His accounting salary gave Knight the steady income he needed to cover his personal costs, invest in the business, and smooth out the inevitable ups and downs in the early days.

Without the financial stability from his day job, Knight may have had to abandon his entrepreneurial pursuit or take costly loans to sustain the venture.

After nearly five years of sacrificing nights and weekends to build his company, Knight had developed enough proof of concept and revenue to finally feel confident leaving his accounting career.

That ample financial runway allowed Nike the time needed to refine designs, build demand, and cement durable supplier relationships until the business achieved stand-alone profitability.

Phil Knight's story clearly demonstrates that even visionary entrepreneurs need steady income and savings while launching new ventures. Having a financial runway provides that safe landing strip to pursue your dreams without crashing.

A more important aspect of a financial runway is it provides invaluable peace of mind. It—

- Allows taking smart risks. With sufficient savings as a buffer, you can confidently take calculated risks needed to start a business, like leaving a secure job, without jeopardizing basic financial needs.
- Covers costs if plans fall through. Things rarely go perfectly according to plan when starting out. A strong runway gives you time to pivot if sales are slower than expected without immediately tapping retirement savings or accruing debt.
- Avoids desperate financial decisions. When funds run low, people are more prone to making hasty, risky

financial choices out of desperation. A healthy runway prevents you from accepting bad terms with partners or investors.

- Provides time to wait for the right opportunities. Having your basic needs covered for a period allows you to thoughtfully consider options and wait for deals or partnerships that are the right fit rather than feeling pressured.
- Allows focus on the business. Financial stress is mentally and emotionally taxing, draining important time and energy away from refining your business operations and offerings. With those basic needs met, you can channel that energy more productively.
- Fuels motivation and confidence. Having evidence that you've planned prudently and have funds to pursue your vision boosts motivation and self-belief that you can succeed, especially during difficult early days.

Having ample financial runway provides vital peace of mind when launching a new venture. But belt-tightening may be required before take-off to extend that runway. As you prepare to leave a stable career for unpredictable self-employment, reining in spending on non-essentials could maximize your savings runway. Though not always easy, limiting lifestyle expenses demonstrates commitment to your vision.

Now that we've addressed the importance of having a financial runway, let's discuss practical ways to economize your lifestyle in the lead-up to entrepreneurship. Cutting back discretionary spending helps prolong your runway and ensures you can cover basic needs if business income is delayed. Don't worry, your thriftiness is only temporary. Soon you'll be soaring high once your venture takes off!

Lower Your Expense

Back in 2015, the weight of my financial burdens felt like an iron chain dragging me down. The hefty mortgage, the petrol-guzzling BMW X5, and the constant demands of raising three young kids were all conspiring to drain my already struggling career coaching practice. My meagre income barely covered the basics, and money worries became a persistent, gnawing cloud in my mind. They sapped my focus, fuelled impatience, and, frankly, I wouldn't have wanted to be around the 2015 version of myself.

Cost-cutting became my mantra. I knew the impractical luxuries had to go first. The house went on the market, and the BMW was traded for a more affordable, fuel-efficient Japanese car. Selling these felt like shedding heavy weights, a wave of relief washing over me. We downsized to a rental for two years, making do with less space but also significantly less financial strain.

In hindsight, these sacrifices should have been made before launching the venture. While the financial benefits were immediate, the psychological adjustment took time. The cognitive load of learning to live with less added another layer of stress, taking precious energy away from building my business.

Financial prudence isn't just about cutting costs; it's also about making strategic choices. Take Mumpreneur Nancy Lai of A Mighty Venture, for example. While she was on the verge of upgrading to a private condominium, her pre-business priorities shifted. Recognizing the importance of financial security, she opted for the stability of public housing, ensuring a solid foundation for her upcoming venture.

For families like Nancy's, long haul family holidays to Europe might get replaced by nearer countries explored on budget airlines.

So how much financial runway or expense reduction are we talking about?

That begins with your budget.

How to Budget if You Are Self-Employed

With some dedicated time and planning, you can create a budget that covers your business and personal expenses while still funding your dreams and savings goals. Follow this comprehensive guide to budgeting for self-employed success!

Start by estimating your monthly income based on past earnings and projected revenue. Review business records to determine your average monthly income over the last six to twelve months. If you're just starting out, make an educated guess based on market research and expected client contracts. Be conservative here—it's better to pleasantly surprise yourself if you end up earning more than expected down the road.

Whatever number you land on, this will form your income baseline for building the budget. For example, if you earned $4,000 monthly on an average over the past year, use $4,000 as your benchmark for now. You can always adjust later if needed once you refine income projections.

Now comes the fun part—tracking where all your hard-earned money has been going! Make a master list of every business and personal expense. For your business, include things like:

- Equipment, tools, software
- Office or retail space
- Website hosting, domain registration
- Inventory or materials
- Marketing and advertising
- Professional services (e.g. accountant fees)
- Insurance
- Licenses and taxes

For your personal lifestyle, list expenses like:

- Housing (mortgage/rent, property tax, utilities)
- Groceries and dining out

- Insurance (health, home, auto, life)
- Debt repayments (credit cards, loans, etc.)
- Childcare and tuition
- Transportation (lease/loan payments, gas, repairs)
- Cell phone bill
- Memberships and subscriptions

Pro tip: Audit your recurring subscriptions and services closely to spot areas to cut back if needed. For example, pause the wine club membership or Spotify plan during lean financial periods.

This is where the spreadsheet comes in handy! Plug your income baseline and expense estimates into a program like Excel. Then, start allocating portions of your monthly income towards each line item until every dollar is assigned.

Aim to cover business costs first, then essential personal living expenses before discretionary spending. Build in a cushion for savings—at least 10 per cent of income is a good rule of thumb. If your expenses exceed your income, rework the budget to align outgoing and incoming cash flow.

As a business owner, you'll need to pay self-employment taxes. Plan for this significant expense from the start so you don't drain your budget later. How much should you set aside? A good guideline is 20–30 per cent of your income. Use an online calculator to estimate your specific tax liability.

Automate this process by putting aside a percentage of each pay cheque into a designated tax savings account. Come tax time, those funds will be ready to cover your obligation. Nothing stings like owing a huge tax bill you can't afford! Proactive planning prevents a major pitfall.

Having steady income is never guaranteed as an entrepreneur. That's why an emergency savings fund should be top priority when budgeting. Try to set aside at least three to six months' worth of living expenses in a secure, liquid account like a high-yield savings account. This will protect you when business fluctuates.

It can take time to build your reserves, so start small. Setting aside even $200 monthly can quickly accumulate security. Make savings non-negotiable by automating transfers from your checking account to savings as soon as you get paid. Out of sight, out of mind!

One advantage of being your own boss—you can adjust your budget based on financial ebbs and flows. For example, landscapers budget lighter in winter, accountants ramp up during tax season. Make your budget flexible around high- vs low-income periods.

When you enter a slow season, try these tips to reduce expenses temporarily:

- Pause non-essential subscriptions and memberships
- Eat out less, brown bag lunch
- Hold off on new equipment purchases
- Use credit card points for free vacations
- Avoid unnecessary trips and spending
- The key is having a plan in place so you can get lean without stress when needed. Then run full speed ahead when flush periods return!

Building your budget is just step one; the real work comes in living by it. Review your budget monthly to ensure you're sticking to what's realistic for both business and personal finances. Life happens—when needs change, reset your budget numbers right away. Don't wait for the new year to make adjustments.

Technology can simplify this process. Using budgeting apps connects your bank accounts so you can see spending categories and cash flow in real time. Syncing accounts also consolidates statements into one place come tax time.

But don't forget to celebrate your wins. Occasional splurges and treats keep the budget journey fun. Just incorporate these in moderation. For example, after landing a big client, budget a nice dinner out or gadget purchase as a reward for your hard work.

Building rewards into your budget keeps you motivated to stick to your plan and reach those monetary milestones. Just focus treats around accomplishments versus random desires to stay on track financially.

Financial Projection

With expenses sorted and accounted for, it is time to project your potential earnings.

Project Your Revenue

First and foremost, estimate your expected revenue over the next one to three years. Several factors come into play:

If you're an existing business, use previous years' sales data to project growth trends. Is revenue increasing steadily year-over-year? Seasonal?

Research your industry's growth patterns. Is the market expanding or contracting?

Factor in your marketing plans. Will you expand services or products to boost sales?

Consider economic conditions that may impact customers' spending.

Conservatively estimate revenue potential, especially when starting out. It's easier to be pleasantly surprised if you exceed projections than scramble if you fall short.

Forecast Operating Expenses

Next, detail the ongoing expenses required to operate your business at projected sales volumes. This includes:

- Cost of goods sold – Materials, inventory, production costs
- Rent and utilities

- Marketing and advertising
- Insurance
- Accounting and legal fees
- Salaries and wages (if you hire staff)
- Software, tools, equipment costs
- Research and development

Accounting software like FreshBooks[1] can analyse past expenses to intelligently forecast future needs. Budget for a 10–15 per cent cushion for unexpected expenses.

Let's look at the following example:

Jane is a freelance graphic designer who works from home. She decided to make a list of all the items that she needs or uses in her work. She categorized each item into start-up cost or ongoing cost and estimated how much each item will cost her per month or per year. Here is her list:

Item	Cost
Laptop	$1,000
Graphic tablet	$300
Software subscription	$50/month
Printer	$200
Ink cartridges	$30/month
Paper	$10/month
Business cards	$50
Website domain and hosting	$100/year
Total start-up costs	$1,550 + $90/month + $100/year

---

[1] https://www.freshbooks.com/en-sg/

Item	Cost
Electricity	$50/month
Internet	$40/month
Phone	$30/month
Health insurance	$300/month
Liability insurance	$50/month
Income tax	15% of net income
Self-employment tax	15.3% of net income
Professional services	$100/month
Total ongoing costs	$570/month + 30.3% of net income

By making this list, Jane was able to identify her key self-employment and ongoing expenses. She realized that she needed to save up at least $1,550 to cover her start-up costs. She also realized that she needed to earn at least $570 per month plus 30.3 per cent of her net income to cover her ongoing costs.

Exercise: Make a list of your key self-employment and ongoing expenses and estimate how much they will cost you per month or per year.

Project Your Profit Margins

Now estimate your profit margins based on projected revenue minus expenses. This helps determine pricing strategies and cash flow. Be realistic about profit potential in your industry. Many self-employments might not give a return in Year 1.

Let's look at the following example:

John is an online coach who helps people improve their communication skills. He decided to develop his cost estimates and projections for his business using the following steps:

- Estimated his revenue: John estimated that he could charge $100 per hour for his coaching services. He also estimated that he could attract 10 clients per month who would sign up for 4 sessions each. Therefore, he estimated his monthly revenue to be $4,000 ($100 x 10 x 4).

- Estimated his expenses: John estimated his start-up costs and ongoing costs using the list he made in the previous part of this section. He estimated his total start-up costs to be $1,500 and his total ongoing costs to be $1,000 per month.

- Calculated his profit margin: John calculated his monthly profit margin by subtracting his monthly expenses from his monthly revenue and dividing the result by his monthly revenue. He calculated his monthly profit margin to be 75 per cent (($4,000 – $1,000) / $4,000).

- Projected his revenue: John projected his monthly revenue growth by setting a goal of increasing his client base by 10 per cent every month. He also projected his hourly rate growth by setting a goal of increasing his price by 5 per cent every quarter. Therefore, he projected his monthly revenue for the next year using a spreadsheet.

- Projected his expenses: John projected his monthly expense growth by considering any changes or adjustments that he needed to make to his start-up costs and ongoing costs. He projected that he would need to invest another $500 in equipment after six months and another $500 in marketing after nine months. He also projected that he would need to increase his insurance premium by 10 per cent every year. Therefore, he projected his monthly expenses for the next year using a spreadsheet.

- Projected his profit margin: John projected his monthly profit margin by subtracting his projected monthly expenses from his projected monthly revenue and dividing the result by his projected monthly revenue. He projected his monthly profit margin for the next year using a spreadsheet.

Here is John's spreadsheet showing his cost estimates and projections for his online coaching business:

Month	Revenue	Expenses	Profit Margin
1	$4,000	$1,000	75%
2	$4,400	$1,000	77%
3	$4,840	$1,000	79%
4	$5,324	$1,050[2]	80%
5	$5,856	$1,050	82%
6	$6,442	$1,550	76%
7	$7,086	$1,550	78%
8	$7,795	$1,550	80%
9	$8,575	$2,050	76%
10	$9,432	$2,050	78%
11	$10,375	$2,050	80%
12	$11,413	$2,155	81%

_____

[2] Assuming expenses will go up in relation to higher revenue

By developing this spreadsheet, John was able to see how his revenue, expenses, and profit margin would change over time. He was also able to see how much money he needed to make to break even and to achieve his desired income level.

Forecast Your Cash Flow

Cash flow projections help anticipate future cash coming in versus going out monthly. This helps ensure you can cover costs without cash flow gaps that lead to shortfalls or debt.

Incorporate projected sales on accounts receivable and expenses like payroll, taxes, inventory orders, and large purchases. Identify any months where expenses may temporarily outpace revenue to proactively plan and budget accordingly.

Create a Balance Sheet

A balance sheet summarizes business assets, liabilities, and equity at a given point. Projecting this annually helps monitor financial health and net worth.

Assets may include cash, accounts receivable, equipment, and intellectual property. Liabilities cover debts like loans, mortgages, accounts payable. Equity is assets minus liabilities—essentially the solopreneur's stake.

Budget for Unexpected Costs and Contingencies

The third step to crunching the numbers is to budget for unexpected costs and contingencies that may arise in your self-employment venture. These are the costs that you cannot predict or control, but that can have a significant impact on your finances. Some examples of unexpected costs and contingencies are:

- *Emergencies*: These are the costs that you need to pay for dealing with urgent or unforeseen situations, such as accidents, illnesses, natural disasters, or thefts. These may include medical bills, repairs, replacements, or legal fees.
- *Refunds*: These are the costs that you need to pay for returning money to your customers who are dissatisfied with your products or services. These may include processing fees, shipping fees, or lost revenue.
- *Legal fees*: These are the costs that you need to pay for resolving any legal issues or disputes that may arise in your business, such as lawsuits, contracts, trademarks, or patents. These may include attorney fees, court fees, or settlement fees.
- *Changes in market conditions*: These are the costs that you need to pay for adapting to any changes in the demand or supply of your products or services, such as changes in customer preferences, competitor actions, regulations, or technology. These may include research and development costs, marketing costs, or training costs.

To budget for unexpected costs and contingencies, you can use the following steps:

- Estimate the likelihood and impact of each potential cost or contingency. This means assessing how probable and how severe each cost or contingency is for your business. You can use historical data, industry trends, expert opinions, or your own judgment to help you estimate these factors.
- Allocate a percentage of your revenue or profit to a contingency fund. This means setting aside a portion of your income to cover any unexpected costs or contingencies that may occur. You can use a simple rule of thumb, such as 10 per cent of your revenue or profit, or

a more sophisticated formula based on your risk tolerance and financial goals.

- Review and update your budget regularly. This means monitoring your actual performance and comparing it to your projections and assumptions. You can also review and update your estimates of the likelihood and impact of each potential cost or contingency based on new information or feedback. You can use a spreadsheet or an online tool to help you review and update your budget.

Example: How Lisa budgeted for unexpected costs and contingencies for her freelance writing business

Lisa is a freelance writer who works from home. She decided to budget for unexpected costs and contingencies for her business using the following steps:

- Estimate the likelihood and impact of each potential cost or contingency. Lisa identified four main types of unexpected costs and contingencies that could affect her business: emergencies, refunds, legal fees, and changes in market conditions. She estimated the likelihood and impact of each one using a scale from 1 (low) to 5 (high). Here is her table:

Cost/Contingency	Likelihood	Impact
Emergencies	2	4
Refunds	3	3
Legal fees	1	5
Changes in market conditions	4	2

- Allocate a percentage of her revenue or profit to a contingency fund. Lisa decided to allocate 10 per cent of her monthly revenue to a contingency fund. She estimated her monthly revenue to be $5,000 based on her previous work history and current contracts. Therefore, she allocated $500 per month to her contingency fund.
- Review and update her budget regularly. Lisa reviewed and updated her budget every month using a spreadsheet. She tracked her actual revenue and expenses and compared them to her projections and assumptions. She also reviewed and updated her estimates of the likelihood and impact of each potential cost or contingency based on new information or feedback.

Avoid Common Financial Mistakes

The fourth and final step to crunching the numbers is to avoid common financial mistakes that can ruin your self-employment venture. These are the errors or oversights that can lead to inaccurate or incomplete financial information, poor financial decisions, or legal troubles. Some examples of common financial mistakes are:

- Underestimating costs: This is the mistake of not accounting for all the expenses that you will incur as a self-employed person, or underestimating how much they will cost you. This can result in running out of money, losing money, or missing opportunities.
- Overestimating revenue: This is the mistake of being too optimistic or unrealistic about how much money you will earn as a self-employed person, or overestimating how fast or easy it will be to generate revenue. This can result in overspending, overcommitting, or underdelivering.

- Mingling personal and business finances: This is the mistake of not separating your personal and business accounts, transactions, or records. This can result in confusion, inefficiency, or tax problems.
- Ignoring taxes: This is the mistake of not paying attention to your tax obligations and deductions as a self-employed person, or ignoring them until the last minute. This can result in penalties, fines, or audits.
- Neglecting record-keeping: This is the mistake of not keeping track of your income and expenses as a self-employed person, or not keeping them organized and accurate. This can result in errors, omissions, or fraud.

To avoid common financial mistakes, you can use the following tips:

- Use a spreadsheet or an accounting software to help you estimate and project your costs and revenues accurately and realistically.
- Review and update your budget regularly and adjust your actions accordingly.
- Open a separate bank account and credit card for your business and use them exclusively for your business transactions.
- Set aside a percentage of your income for taxes and pay them on time.
- Keep receipts, invoices, bank statements, and other documents that support your income and expenses and store them securely.

Self-employment involves a leap of faith—exchanging security for autonomy and purpose. But to avoid a painful landing, you must diligently account for financial realities.

Crunching the numbers thoroughly upfront provides a sturdy launchpad. Meticulous planning prevents income shortfalls or cash flow gaps mid-flight that can send your venture into a tailspin.

Arm yourself with ample savings to cover launch costs and personal needs until your business generates sustainable profits. Conservatively estimate expenses and revenue, adding cushions for surprises.

Streamline spending and build lean operations that align with early revenue projections. Consider bartering services or partnerships to conserve costs.

Automate billing and accounting using software. Document all transactions meticulously. Keep business and personal finances wholly separate.

Learn tax obligations and leverage deductions strategically. Work with professionals to ensure legal and accounting compliance.

The administrative work may seem tedious next to passion projects. But robust infrastructure allows you to focus energy on higher goals rather than distractions.

With diligent financial planning and discipline, profitability can become self-sustaining over time. Patience and grit will carry you through the turbulent take-off phase.

You are ready for lift-off into purposeful self-employment. So ground yourself in realistic budgets and projections. This gives the freedom to ultimately soar unencumbered by money worries.

The numbers may seem daunting initially. But the pay-off of fulfilment makes the effort worthwhile.

Key Takeaways

- Have enough financial runway (savings) to cover your living expenses for at least six to eighteen months before starting your business.

- Develop a comprehensive budget that covers your business and personal expenses based on realistic income and expense projections.
- Track and categorize all your income and expenses regularly to review actuals versus projections.
- Plan for taxes as a self-employed individual by setting aside 20–30 per cent of income for estimated tax liability.
- Build an emergency fund containing three to six months of living expenses to protect your business from financial fluctuations.
- Adjust your budget temporarily during slow seasons by reducing discretionary spending.
- Create projections for revenue, expenses, profit margins, and cash flow over one to three years to anticipate financial needs.
- Budget 10–15 per cent of expected costs as a contingency fund for unexpected expenses.
- Keep personal and business finances separate for clarity and tax purposes.
- Consult accounting tools and professionals to ensure accurate record-keeping and compliance.
- Thoroughly research your industry to base projections on realistic assumptions.
- Avoid underestimating costs and overestimating revenue when planning.

Chapter 6

Building Your Personal Brand

'Your personal brand is what people say about you when you're not in the room.'

—Jeff Bezos

We all start somewhere on the journey to establishing our personal brand. This chapter shares my own twists and turns to help you avoid pitfalls as you define what makes you stand out.

Before we dive into my story, it's important to level-set on what personal branding entails and why it matters, especially for the self-employed. Your personal brand is essentially your reputation—it's how you are perceived based on the image you project consistently over time through your experiences, expertise, values, and communication style.

Developing a strong personal brand allows you to stand out, build authority in your niche, and attract ideal opportunities. For the self-employed, defining your distinctive brand helps you connect with the right customers and partners. It enables you to cut through noise and establish trust as the go-to person for what you do best.

Just look at renowned personal brands like Oprah, Gary Vaynerchuk, or Marie Forleo who've built empires around their reputations. Or experts like Michael Hyatt and Seth

Godin who are synonymous with leadership and marketing respectively. Investing in your brand early pays dividends for years to come.

The Accidental Blogger

My initial motivation for blogging across a variety of topics like recruitment, career advice, entrepreneurship, and even parenting? I simply enjoyed writing and connecting with any audience that found my content interesting or helpful.

At first a hobby, I eventually had too many blogs to maintain: my main site, plus careerladder.sg and myfuntasticfour.com. The work of writing quality content in so many areas quickly became unsustainable. I was spreading myself thin.

The Tipping Point

A friend interested in HR tech investing suggested I double down on that niche. My other topics had more obvious experts, but HR tech was wide open here. This prompted an epiphany—I needed to focus.

While it was painful to let go of blogs tied to previous passions, I could now direct all energy into a niche where I spotted opportunity. After reflecting on my experiences, HR tech felt like the right path forward.

Establishing Myself as 'the' HR Tech Person

I set out interviewing and profiling local HR tech start-ups, sharing insights from founders themselves. This kicked off my first HR tech market map for Singapore in 2017, connecting and cross-promoting ecosystem players.

This is the 2018 version of the map, which expanded
into more than 100+ companies.

The market map gained viral traction across the industry. I continued updating it annually as a go-to resource. Speaking engagements and guest articles ensued.

Within a couple years, I'd organically become the HR tech guru in Singapore. Media and new start-ups came to me as the authority. My focused content and outreach laid the foundations.

Of course, zeroing in on HR tech earlier would have saved time spent on irrelevant topics. But through trial and error, I learned how powerful niche focus can be in branding.

Key Lessons on Finding Your Brand

While our journeys differ, here are core lessons applicable to any solopreneur's path:

1. Assess your strengths and interests, then match those to an underserved niche. Avoid overcrowded areas where standing out is difficult. An adjacent space may be your breakout opportunity.
2. Resist spreading yourself too thin. While tempting to show range, laser focus wins in branding. Find your one defining niche and own it completely.
3. Measure traction once you zero in on a niche. Analyse what content and activities gain the most momentum. Double down on those to accelerate your positioning.
4. Don't become discouraged by early failures or course corrections. Refining your brand takes experimenting and patience. With consistent effort, people will take notice.

Now equipped with my hard-won lessons, let's explore key steps to finding and amplifying your own distinctive brand.

Defining Your Value Proposition

With niche focus established, the next crucial branding task is dialling in your unique value proposition (UVP). Your UVP is a clear, memorable statement that conveys the specific value you provide target customers.

Crafting my UVP was an iterative process of trial and error. Early attempts to differentiate myself missed the mark or were too confusing. After refining based on feedback and testing, my current UVP came into focus: 'I help growth-stage HR tech vendors generate sustainable pipeline.' The outcomes are clearer for my audience—qualified leads and revenue growth.

This positions me as a preferred partner for a specific customer profile, rather than simply types of roles I fill. The difference between those two approaches became obvious once I developed a value proposition that resonated.

In defining your own UVP, resist the temptation to list credentials or capabilities. Instead, focus on who you help and the end result they desire. You can use this simple formula:

[I help] [target customer] [achieve a desired outcome] [by providing something of value].

For example: 'I help busy professionals feel less stressed by teaching customizable mindfulness techniques.'

Here are some additional examples of compelling value propositions:

- I help overwhelmed moms simplify parenting by providing customized daily routines to reduce stress and chaos.
- I help introverted entrepreneurs become confident public speakers by providing proven presentation training tailored to their personality strengths.
- I help companies improve employee retention by conducting in-depth culture audits and implementing data-driven strategies.

- I help busy couples reignite romance by designing personalized date nights full of new shared experiences.
- I help restaurants drive more reservations by optimizing their online presence and implementing digital marketing best practices.
- I help teams collaborate better by facilitating open communication workshops focused on conflict resolution and trust-building.
- I help new realtors jump-start their business by providing one-on-one coaching and connections to my network of brokerages and lenders.
- I help working women find fulfilment by teaching them to set aligned personal, professional, and financial goals tailored to what matters most.
- I help aspiring authors get published by providing ghostwriting and book publishing services based on their unique stories.

The key is highlighting the target customer, their struggle or desire, and how you can deliver a solution tailored to their needs. The value proposition frames the transformation you provide.

A compelling yet concise UVP provides direction for all branding and marketing activities to follow. Get this right first and your personal brand will magnetically attract the perfect next steps.

Promoting Your Brand Identity

Now that your niche speciality and value proposition are established, consistent branding reinforces them across touchpoints.

With these in place, I ensured my website, social media, speaking engagements, and other materials aligned. The goal was immersing my audience in a consistent experience reflecting my brand.

For example, when I began speaking at HR tech conferences, my presentation templates incorporated the same colours, logo, and messaging as my other assets. This created instant familiarity and reinforced my positioning.

Consistency catalyses the 'rule of seven' for branding. The more touchpoints where you project alignment, the faster your niche identity takes root in your market.

Experiment to find visuals, language, and concepts that click with your goals. Reuse them widely to imprint your brand effectively. The payoff will be prospects who remember and relate to you.

Key Takeaways

- Developing a strong personal brand is important for self-employed individuals to stand out, build authority, and attract the right opportunities and clients. It establishes trust as the go-to expert in your niche.

- The author initially blogged about various topics for fun but realized he needed to niche down to focus his effort and branding. He chose to specialize in HR tech where he saw opportunity.

- Defining a clear and memorable unique value proposition (UVP) that communicates the specific value you provide targets is important for branding. The author refined his UVP through testing and feedback.

- Using consistent branding and messaging across all touchpoints like website, social media, presentations, etc. helps immerse audiences and reinforce your niche positioning faster through repetition.

- Experimenting and finding visuals, language, and concepts that resonate for your goals is important. Reusing them widely imprints your brand effectively in the market over time. Niche focus combined with consistent branding builds authority.

Chapter 7

LinkedIn Mastery

'LinkedIn is the world's largest professional network. Use it to your advantage.'

—Melanie Dodaro

If you recall in chapter one, my life turned 180 degrees within twenty-four hours of a LinkedIn post. It was a call-out (although more of an SOS to me at that time) to let the world know that I'm going independent and would be open to engagements.

A day later, I was looking at three assignments that would collectively help me generate more revenue per month than I did from my previous pay check.

And it wasn't one-off?

I have since secured speaking gigs, writing assignments, video production work, and more. All these would not have been possible if I had not utilized LinkedIn to build my personal branding and my thought leadership.

With over 850 million members, LinkedIn is the indispensable platform for establishing your personal brand and extending yourself as a thought leader. I've grown my own following to over 40,000 connections, enabling me to amplify my personal brand and my former recruiting business.

While I operate in B2B, LinkedIn is equally valuable for personal branding whether you sell to consumers or other businesses. The same best practices apply.

Importantly the world of selling has evolved a fair bit. Even companies with BDR (Business Development Reps) teams are floundering. This is according to Adam Robinson, the CEO at Retention.com on one of his LinkedIn post[1]. He added that the future of selling is making yourself an influencer. The thirty founders he spoke with are all telling him that founder brand content creates tons of leads.

Granted one can be an influencer on any social media platform, I will be sticking to LinkedIn as that is the space I operate on.

But before we get to that, let's make sure you get the fundamentals correct. To begin with, you need to make sure that your profile is complete and Creator mode ready (more on that later).

Are you ready for my LinkedIn Masterclass?

Let's go.

Headline Crafting: An Effective LinkedIn Headline in 120 Characters or Less

Crafting an effective LinkedIn headline in 120 characters or less can be challenging. It's tempting to just use LinkedIn's default of your current job title. But a customized, strategic headline helps you stand out and catches the attention of prospects and recruiters scrolling through search results.

Your headline appears right next to your profile photo on LinkedIn. So it serves as a first impression and your personal billboard, making those limited 120 characters valuable real

---

[1] https://www.linkedin.com/posts/retentionadam_ive-spoken-to-30-founders-over-the-past-activity-7100875351341346827-Vchd

estate. Simply accepting LinkedIn's generic headline is a missed opportunity to showcase your differentiated capabilities, accomplishments, and value.

Some tips for crafting a stellar LinkedIn headline to represent you:

- Focus on conveying your unique value proposition and how you help clients in a compelling way. Accompany it with a high quality, professional profile photo for maximum impact. If the unique value proposition you created before works within the wordcount, you can just copy and paste over.

- Avoid overly vague, generic, or hyperbolic language. Be clear and benefit-driven but not overtly self-promotional or boastful.

- Strategically use keywords and phrases your target audience would search to find you. This helps attract the right prospects.

- Succinctly describe how you improve customers' lives or businesses. Explain your impact in simple, relatable terms.

- Skip internal jargon or niche concepts those outside your field won't grasp. Distil your message down to layman's terms.

- Feature relevant accolades, credentials, or media mentions if possible to lend credibility.

- Recognize the headline doesn't need to cram in every accomplishment. Prioritize the most important elements for your goals and audience.

To generate initial headline ideas, use a headline generator tool like ResumeWorded.com. Then carefully customize and refine the results to optimally represent your personal brand and attract your ideal opportunities.

The Power of a Quality LinkedIn Headshot

Having an authentic, professional headshot on LinkedIn makes you seem more real and approachable in the virtual world. Some people don't take it seriously, but a poor quality, distracting, or missing headshot can significantly undermine your ability to connect with others.

The ideal solution is investing in a headshot taken by an experienced professional photographer. But if that's not possible, here are some tips for taking a decent DIY LinkedIn headshot yourself:

- Don't simply use a casual selfie or cropped/zoomed-in images with missing head/body parts. Save the informal selfies for Instagram instead.
- Don't overlay your headshot with a logo or graphic that detracts focus from your face and humanity. Let yourself shine.
- Don't use an irrelevant group photo. LinkedIn is for professional networking, not Facebook.

- Don't leave your headshot blank or use LinkedIn's silhouette as a placeholder. This makes you seem dubious and sketchy.
- Avoid busy, distracting backgrounds that pull attention away from you. Simple and clean backdrops are best.
- If you already have a quality headshot photo but with a cluttered background, use an AI-powered profile picture maker like pfpmaker.com to seamlessly remove the background and replace it with something clean and professional looking.

The key is looking polished, credible, and approachable. Investing in a professional headshot is ideal if possible. But you can still DIY an effective LinkedIn photo for free using profile photo editing tools. Go to pfpmaker.com to instantly transform your existing photo by removing and replacing the background.

A proper, high-quality headshot makes you seem more relatable, trustworthy, and engaging. It's worth the effort to maximize your LinkedIn presence and personal brand.

Crafting a Compelling LinkedIn Summary

Your LinkedIn summary section is essentially your professional bio—the first few paragraphs right below your name and current job titles. This crucial space allows you to introduce and distinguish yourself beyond just listing job titles and employers.

An engaging, well-written summary makes a stellar first impression, strategically highlighting your accomplishments, skills, and expertise in a concise, scannable way. It also reveals a bit of your personality so readers gain a sense of what to expect when potentially contacting you for opportunities.

When drafting your summary, write in an authentic first-person voice using 'I' statements. Keep it relatively short and skimmable—approximately four to five tight paragraphs of one to two sentences each. And be sure to thoroughly proofread for any errors.

A distinct, memorable summary combines authenticity and a dash of creativity. Helpful sections to include:

- OPENING LINE: What's the very first thing you want people to know about you? Grab their attention.
- PITCH: Explain why you're a rising star in your field using keywords. Talk about your passions, superpowers, and points of differentiation.
- CALL-TO-ACTION: Wrap up your summary with a clear call-to-action about what you want readers to do after viewing your profile.
- PROOF: Attach work samples, testimonials, or relevant links below your summary section to provide credibility and showcase your abilities.

Tools like Grammarly, Hemingway Editor, and ResumeWorded's LinkedIn summary generator can aid in crafting clear, compelling summaries. Start by brainstorming a draft then refine and tighten it up.

The goal is crafting a personalized, engaging overview showcasing your best qualities and achievements. Take the time to make a strong first impression and convey your value with your LinkedIn summary.

Strategies for Gathering Convincing LinkedIn Testimonials

Testimonials and recommendations from others build immense credibility on your LinkedIn profile. When colleagues, employers, or clients publicly endorse your skills and expertise, it carries much more weight than you simply making those claims yourself.

Here are some proactive strategies for gathering stellar testimonials and recommendations:

- Ask past managers and employers for LinkedIn recommendations—from your direct boss to showcase you were a great employee, and from co-workers to show you were an amazing colleague.
- Get testimonials from satisfied clients, especially right after successfully completing a project when it's fresh. Offer to return the favour.
- Digitize any existing written recommendations or references you already have and proactively ask those contacts to post them on LinkedIn.

Testimonials are invaluable for social proof on your LinkedIn profile. Use these proactive tactics to gather convincing recommendations from others that reinforce your expertise.

Unlocking LinkedIn Creator Mode to Boost Your Influence

Activating LinkedIn's Creator Mode gives you access to powerful tools to expand your reach and establish your authority as an industry expert. Turning on this setting provides key benefits like:

- Appearing in LinkedIn's search, topic, and discovery results, allowing your content to be discovered and seen by people interested in your niche, even without existing first-degree connections.
- Gaining more engaged followers – Consistently highlighting your expertise through original content helps attract an audience that wants to keep learning from you. Publishing on specific topics and using relevant hashtags lets people easily find, understand, and choose to follow you.
- Accessing creator analytics – Using specialized tools to track performance of your original content, establish your unique thought leadership voice, and inform your content strategy.

When you flip the switch to become a LinkedIn Creator, your profile changes in key ways:

- The standard Connect button switches to a Follow button.
- You display your number of followers prominently.
- You can showcase top topics as hashtags for discoverability.
- Your original content is highlighted and showcased at the top above work experience.
- You may be suggested for others to follow based on your niche.

To activate LinkedIn Creator Mode:

- In your profile, go to your account dashboard and toggle the Creator Mode switch on.
- Then select one to five defining topics that best represent your expertise.

Congratulations! You're now unlocked as a LinkedIn Creator. Use these new features and analytics to grow your audience reach and establish your thought leadership. The key is proactively enabling creator mode to access tools for expanding your influence.

How to Know if You Are on the Right Track?

One way to measure your effectiveness using LinkedIn for branding and networking is through their Social Selling Index (SSI). This index evaluates factors like the strength of your profile, how well you engage with content, the quality of your network, and your relationship-building efforts.

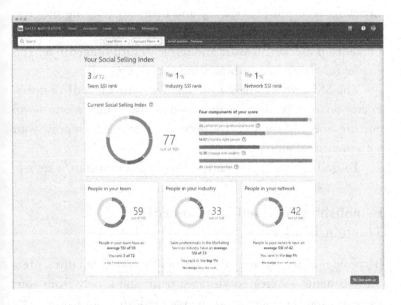

Industry leaders aim for an SSI score of at least 75, with over 80 considered high mastery of using LinkedIn to network and promote your brand. The SSI dashboard allows you to view your score and compare against industry peers, illuminating areas for improvement.

Some best practices for boosting your SSI include:

- Regularly share your own content and insights through posts, articles, and comments.
- Have a complete, optimized profile that builds your professional brand.
- Comment and engage thoughtfully with others' posts beyond just liking.
- Use search to find and connect with ideal prospects and partners.
- Connect with those who create content you find valuable.

Checking your SSI periodically and manually tracking progress over time allows you to benchmark and steadily enhance your LinkedIn presence. Measure and refine to turn LinkedIn into an engine for your personal brand and network growth.

The SSI provides data to maximize your LinkedIn impact. Focus on quality over quantity—not just vanity metrics—to nurture the meaningful connections that will support your entrepreneurial journey.

To find your SSI, go to https://www.linkedin.com/sales/ssi.

Establishing Yourself as a LinkedIn Thought Leader

Becoming a recognized thought leader on LinkedIn offers many benefits—increased visibility, trust, and loyalty from your audience, and the ability to shape your industry. But who exactly is a thought leader?

A thought leader is an expert who generates and distributes valuable insights and perspectives. They attract opportunities by showcasing their knowledge. Thought leaders educate and inspire audiences by challenging assumptions and introducing innovative ideas.

For me, the path to becoming a recognized thought leader started gradually as I enjoyed writing and began using LinkedIn early on. I started out by sharing career tips and recruitment insights through posts. After LinkedIn introduced their article option, I published more of my long-form content. Over time, this led to increased visibility and traffic. I eventually gained accolades like being named an AIHR Global HR Influencer. These small wins snowballed, opening doors for job opportunities, selling my LinkedIn course, and booking high-profile guests for my podcast.

While competition has increased, I've stayed focused on providing value through authenticity. This has nurtured meaningful connections that sparked new possibilities I never imagined. For instance, sharing vulnerable reflections on my mother's passing led to heart-warming messages from strangers turned friends.

LinkedIn thought leadership compounds, but you have to find your unique voice. If you can add value consistently, a community forms around shared interests. Nurture this, and the platform can connect you to life-changing relationships and chances you never expected.

To become a LinkedIn thought leader, you need to:

- Produce high-quality content regularly in various formats like blogs, videos, podcasts, carousel, newsletter, or simply a text post. Demonstrate your expertise while providing solutions.
- Avoid excessive self-promotion. Focus on serving your audience with authenticity and humility.
- Engage actively with your community by responding to feedback, joining discussions, collaborating with peers.
- Continuously expand your knowledge. Seek ways to improve through feedback.

Understanding LinkedIn's algorithm is key to maximizing reach and engagement as a thought leader. Relevance, timing, clear calls-to-action, and consistency impact how your content performs.

Post when your audience is active on weekdays. Use relevant keywords. Encourage engagement with clear CTAs. Post consistently but avoid oversaturation.

Becoming a thought leader takes time but compounds your authority. Educate and inspire your community of followers with high-value insights. Listen and engage authentically. With a thoughtful LinkedIn strategy, you can establish yourself as an industry leader.

Establishing yourself as a thought leader on LinkedIn can be especially beneficial if you are self-employed or running your own business. As an entrepreneur without the brand recognition of a major company behind you, demonstrating your expertise is crucial for attracting clients and opportunities.

Thought leadership allows you to showcase your unique experience and perspectives, making you stand out in a crowded market. It humanizes your personal brand, building the trust and relationships vital for independent professionals to succeed. Self-employed individuals often rely heavily on digital platforms like LinkedIn for networking and lead generation. Becoming a recognized leader in your niche gives you added credibility and influence with ideal prospects and partners. The inbound opportunities generated by thought leadership provide fuel for sustainable self-employment in the digital age.

In the following section, I will break down the practical steps you need to embark on becoming a thought leader.

Let's start by looking at the types of content you can consider:

Crafting Shareable LinkedIn Content

There are three main content angles to leverage for engaging LinkedIn posts:

- Industry Insights – Commentary combining relevant news with your unique perspective and opinion. Provide analysis on current events in your field.

Devadas Krishnadas is a master in industry insights as he breaks down the most complex report into bite-sized, 'why-it-matters' knowledge for every single reader.[2]

For industry insights, go beyond reporting news. Add value by sharing your point of view on the implications.

- Storytelling – Authentic stories from your experiences—behind the scenes, failures, challenges. Make it personal and reveal your journey.

LinkedIn Top Voice Juliana Chan often shares her participation at events and the people she got to know.[3]

[2] https://www.linkedin.com/in/devadas-krishnadas-472b591b2/

[3] https://www.linkedin.com/in/julianachanphd/

For storytelling, don't gloss over the unfiltered realities. The rawness and honesty of your stories will resonate.

- Relatable – Humour, passions, empathy—content that helps people connect through shared interests or struggles.

The late lawyer Adrian Tan is a master in this and often goes by the hypothetical persona 'If I were the King of Singapore' to discuss trending topics with lots of relatable humour.[4]

Besides humour, empathy is also another angle to explore. That was the hallmark of one of Sabrina Ooi's post as she talked about her mental health journey.[5]

For relatable content, tap into what makes you human—causes you care about, hobbies, charity work. Find common ground.

For a start, identify top creators who may be successful on LinkedIn and is most similar to what you are positioning yourself as. For example, if I am running my own leadership coaching practice, I would follow Eric Partaker (one of the most popular coaches on LinkedIn) and review his content.

You can then deconstruct their posts to reverse engineer effective templates.

If you are unsure who to follow, you can also check and ask connections for who to follow as examples. This may surface your interests and direction.

Analyse what content styles perform best and why. Then apply those proven frameworks through your own unique lens. Matching types to your strengths create authenticity that engages audiences.

There is no one 'right' option. Test content angles tailored to you to make the biggest impact on LinkedIn.

---

[4] https://www.linkedin.com/in/tanadrian/
[5] https://www.linkedin.com/in/sabrinaooi/

Hook Matters

Whether you decide to do stories, post critical opinions or simply to share a joke, your hook matters. Hook is a marketing term and it refers to the initial contact with the content that hooks you in.

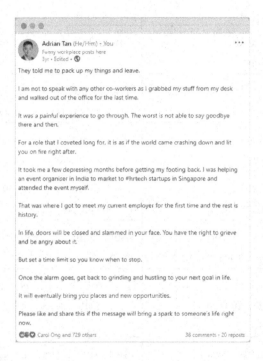

On LinkedIn, that would be the first sentence.[6] It is designed to elicit emotions from your readers so they will be interested to click in, read more, and linger on your post. That will increase the probability of their liking or commenting, both are signals for LinkedIn to prioritize your content to a larger audience and let the flywheel effects kick in.

---

[6] https://www.linkedin.com/posts/adriantanck_hrtech-activity-671405 9776004780032-D1c6?utm_source=share&utm_medium=member_desktop

Here are twenty hooks you can use as reference (Mewborn, n.d.):

Hook	Example
The best way to . . . [desired result]	The best way to build your personal brand on LinkedIn
Why [something] isn't enough	Why cold calling isn't enough
Here's how I . . . and how you can too	Here's how I generate leads on LinkedIn and how you can too
Three ways to quickly . . . [desired result]	Three ways to quickly grow your network on LinkedIn
How to stop [negative problem]	How to stop wasting time on LinkedIn
You'll want to know this hack for . . . [desired result]	You'll want to know this hack for getting noticed on LinkedIn
If you want to . . . [desired result], then here's what to do	If you want to be seen as an expert, then here's what to do
Three simple ways to . . . [desired result] without [negative thing]	Three simple ways to build relationships without being salesy
I NEED NON - [type] to understand . . .	I NEED non-recruiters to understand this LinkedIn strategy
Three reasons why [wrong solution] won't work	Three reasons why spamming connection requests won't work

This is why your [problem] isn't working	This is why your LinkedIn profile isn't working
Here's something REALLY important that [type] should've been taught . . .	Here's something REALLY important that LinkedIn users should've been taught . . .
The #1 thing I tell [type] who wants [result] is this!	The #1 thing I tell introverts who want connections is this!
Listen up if you want to [desired controversial outcome]	Listen up if you want to automate your LinkedIn outreach
How I got [ideal result] in [timeframe]	How I got 500 connections in one week
I don't know who needs to hear this but you're probably [action] wrong	I don't know who needs to hear this but you're probably messaging people wrong
This is one of the most underrated [things]	This is one of the most underrated LinkedIn features
Here's another [type] trick, I guarantee you didn't know	Here's another influencer trick on LinkedIn I guarantee you didn't know
I bought it so you don't have to . . . part [number]	I read this LinkedIn marketing book so you don't have to . . . part 5

The key is using compelling story hooks upfront to draw readers in. Then deliver your message through a condensed story format for LinkedIn.

Leveraging Writing Templates to Streamline Content Creation

Implementing writing templates can provide helpful frameworks to make creating high-quality content more efficient and consistent as an entrepreneur.

The main benefits of using pre-determined writing templates include:

- Easier to follow an established structure instead of starting from scratch.
- Helps improve the quality and flow of your writing.
- Enables consistency that is key for regular content creation.
- Saves time compared to always ideating content from nothing.
- Allows you to focus purely on plugging in the stories and expertise rather than structure.

For example, the popular Morning Brew newsletter uses this effective template:

- Intro paragraph clearly explaining the main topic.
- Zoom in and dig deeper into key details.
- Cite relevant data, statistics, or facts to build credibility.
- Touch on related subtopics or angles.
- Share big picture perspective on why this topic matters.

Of course, other options like telling a personal story, sharing mistakes and lessons learned, myth-busting common misconceptions, step-by-step how-tos, Q&As, etc. can all work too.

There are many writing templates to choose from and new ones are created as you read this. Here are three of them that work well for me.

Template #1 – Personal Story

The personal story template shares a meaningful experience and takeaway. Parts to consider:

- Opening: Share a significant moment to set the scene. Describe that time of life.
- Middle: Explain why you wanted to change. What did that change represent? What did you hope would happen?
- Bridge: In one sentence, say if you were right or wrong.
- Middle: What actually happened after the change? Any unintended consequences? How were things different?
- Close: The moral—what can others learn from your experience?

You don't need every element. The key is outlining a personal story and meaningful reflection.

For example, I shared failing an exam but learning resilience and appreciating hard work.

Adrian Tan (He/Him)
B2B Marketing Strategist | Future of Work Writer | Top 60 Global HR Tech Infl...
1yr • Edited •

Saddest day of my life as I was told to repeat secondary three at Hai Sing Catholic School. It hits me hard when the new term began and my usual friends continue in sec four while I familiarise with a new group of people.

It was worse a year later when most I know moved on to poly.

Self-esteem was at the lowest and I thought that would be the mark of my life story.

But like many life hurdles, it isn't the end but merely a nudge to prepare you for what's next.

It taught me hard work, persistence and rejection. And all these can come together to make success.

So whatever shit you are going through now, as long as you learn from it, things will eventually turn out fine.

Another story told of being fired but not dwelling on it and moving forward (see screenshot on page 119).

Both used a dramatic opening as the hook.

Practise crafting a post on a significant experience. Share your life lessons through storytelling.

Template #2 – Mistakes and Lessons

The mistake and lesson template frames a problem, explains why it matters, and shares what was learned.

- Opening: Describe the mistake. Set the scene—where were you, with whom, what happened?
- Middle: Discuss the lesson learned and advice for readers. Use bullets for actionable takeaways.
- Bridge: Refer back to the original mistake.
- End: Share words of encouragement and key learnings.

Again, you don't need every element. The goal is outlining a meaningful mistake and reflection.

For example, I shared a story about being promoted too soon when starting my career. I didn't handle people taking advantage of me. The opportunity was removed.

In hindsight, it was a blessing. I learned to better manage people. Things happen for a reason.

Eventually, the manager found out. The team member(s) were reprimanded, and my IC role was taken away.

It was demoralizing, and future attempts to seek redemption (and another opportunity) were brushed away.

I was sore and angry af. How could management not give me another chance, and how could my team members foil my promotion opportunity.

But as I looked back with decades of experience behind me, the 20-year-old me did not deserve the chance.

Even if things went well, I most likely would screw it up.

I never had the chance the manage others. Just because a title is bestowed, it will not miraculously be downloaded into my brain.

Painful as it was, it was an indicator that I was inadequate to perform that function.

And it took many more years of study and practice to be decent at it.

The study and practice may never happen if I had succeeded back then; thinking that I had a natural talent to become a supervisor and leading to a worse fiasco at later stages of my career.

Low points in life may not entirely be a bad thing. It may be just what you need to avoid a larger fumble in the future.

Practise crafting a post on a mistake you made and the lesson you learned. Let your errors become meaningful reflections for others.

Template #3 – Myth Template

The myth template frames incorrect assumptions in your industry and debunks them.

- Opening: State the myth and explain its context—how did this false belief arise?
- Middle: Debunk the myth. Use personal stories, stats, or studies as concrete proof.
- Bridge: Transition to what people should be doing instead.
- End: Remind readers the trap of this myth, and there's a better approach.

For example, I shared the myth of needing endless interview rounds for jobs.

I cited an article about someone going through nine rounds.

I debunked it by questioning why this practice persists despite new assessment tools.

I polled readers on better interview round numbers and got great engagement.

Brainstorm myths in your workplace or industry. Then practise creating a post to reveal the truth. Let your insights enlighten people operating under false assumptions or dated beliefs.

Test Different Frameworks to See What Resonates

The key is picking a template that enables you to consistently create engaging, high-quality content without always starting from a blank page. Establish an assembly line for content creation.

Leverage the templates to minimize writer's block. Streamline writing to promote consistency.

Pro tip: If you prefer to shortcut this process, you can check out https://mentis.gg/. At the time of writing, this tool is in beta and hence it is free.

When Do You Post?

We are really going into the nitty-gritty here. Why is the timing of your post important? Just imagine if your audience is in Southeast Asia. It will not make sense for you to push a post out at 2 a.m. since most people would be asleep.

Even if you were to post it during the daytime, there are things to consider. For instance, if you are targeting working professionals, most people would be clearing inboxes on Monday morning and won't have bandwidth to check LinkedIn.

Social media management platform Hootsuite did a study and found that the best times to post are 7.45 a.m., 10.45 a.m., 12.45 p.m., and 5.45 p.m. (Britny Kutuchief, 2023). These are likely the timings when people are commuting, taking breaks, or finishing work. However, these are based on studies done in another country, so you may want to adjust them accordingly. Generally, the best day for B2B posts is Wednesday, followed by Tuesday. For B2C posts, Monday and Wednesday are the best days.

I personally use another social media management platform Buffer to schedule my posts. As you can see, my posts go out on Tuesday, Wednesday, and Thursday at 10.01 a.m.

Your posting schedule for Adrian Tan

Timezone   Stop all posts from being sent on this channel? Learn more

| Singapore - Singapore | | Pause Queue |

Add a new posting time

| Every Day ∨ | Choose times | 10 | 00 | AM | | Add Posting Time |

Posting times ❶   Clear all Posting Times

Monday	Tuesday	Wednesday	Thursday	Friday	Saturday	Sunday
Off	On	On	On	Off	Off	Off
	10 : 01 AM	10 : 01 AM	10 : 01 AM			

This way, I don't have to worry about the exact time to create and post my content. I can just push it to Buffer and let it handle the rest.

Don't Forget Your CTA

Ever clicked a button that says 'Sign Up Now' or 'Download Free Guide'? Those are calls to action, or, in short, CTAs. They're the little nudges marketers use to guide you towards taking the next step they want you to take, whether it's buying something, subscribing to a newsletter, or simply learning more. They can be bold and direct like 'Buy Now', or more subtle like 'Read More', but their goal is always the same: to get you to engage and move forward in the desired direction.

On LinkedIn, CTA could be to reiterate what you do, to encourage interactions to your post or to follow you.

LinkedIn influencer Jasmin Alić is a huge proponent of ending each of his post with a P.S.[7]

In this other example, Singapore LinkedIn influencer David Wee always end off his post to encourage readers to follow him.[8]

Some other possible CTAs are:

- Would you like more of such topics? Send me a direct message or private message.
- What does this mean to you? Comment below.
- Do you know anyone who may find this interesting? Please tag them.

LinkedIn Automation

If you follow enough LinkedIn influencers, you get a sense that you need to do three posts a day, spend hours crafting each of them, and half a day interacting with people.

I do believe that will influence the algorithm enough to make you stand out but I also recognize most of us have business to run.

This is where automation comes in to help reduce the cognitive and administrative burden. These automation tools allow you to systemize and scale key social selling activities on the platform. There are many options available, but some popular automation tools include:

- LeadConnect[9] – Enables sending mass connection requests and messages. Provides statistics on response rates.

---

[7] https://www.linkedin.com/in/alicjasmin/

[8] https://www.linkedin.com/in/david-wee-1618a49a/

[9] https://leadconnect.io/

- ReplyMind[10] – Generates thoughtful, authentic replies to LinkedIn posts and comments.
- Mentis[11] – AI-powered tool to generate LinkedIn post ideas and content.
- Magical[12] – Text expander and data transfer automation for LinkedIn and other sites.

For example, I use LeadConnect to reach out at scale when sharing new content like whitepapers. As you can see in this screenshot, I was able to connect with over 1,000 prospects in Singapore alone, plus hundreds more in Malaysia and Indonesia.

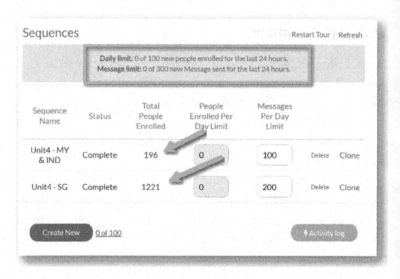

Using such an automated outreach tool will allow you to cast a much wider net and engage audiences that would be impossible to reach manually. However, you still need thoughtful targeting

[10] https://replymind.com/

[11] https://mentis.gg/

[12] https://www.getmagical.com/

and relevant messaging to avoid spam. Most tools have a monthly fee, but can provide great ROI if used properly.

The key is finding the right balance of automation and personalization. Test different tools and strategies to augment (but not entirely replace) one-to-one social selling. With the right approach, automation can significantly amplify your LinkedIn presence and inbound opportunities.

Experiment with leading automation tools like ReplyMind and Mentis to systemize outreach while still maintaining quality. Scale your reach without sacrificing relevance. Let automation enhance your human touch to boost LinkedIn networking and lead generation.

Advanced Analytics

You can't improve what you can't measure. Which brings us to the final section and that is LinkedIn Analytics.

You may have seen the analytics that LinkedIn provides, such as how many views, likes, and comments your posts get, and where your audience comes from. These are useful to identify what works and what doesn't work for your content. You can use this data to make informed decisions about what to post and how to improve your engagement.

However, the analytics that LinkedIn offers are very limited. For example, how do you know which of your posts performed the best out of 200 posts? How do you compare the performance of different types of posts, such as stories, how-tos, or book summaries? How do you track the trends and patterns of your posts over time?

This is where advanced analytics come in handy. They can give you more insights and details about your posts and your audience. One of the tools that I use for this is Shield app.[13]

---

[13] https://www.shieldapp.ai/

Shield app is a third-party application that integrates with your LinkedIn account and gives you more data and features.

For instance, Shield app can show you the trendlines of your views, likes, shares, and comments over time. It can also show you your most popular posts and rank them by different metrics. It can help you to analyse the factors that make your posts successful or unsuccessful.

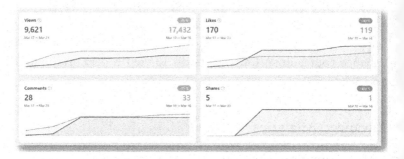

For example, my most popular post was on 11 September 2020 and it got 170,000+ views. It was a personal story about how I failed my exams and how I overcame it. It had a hook, a picture, a theme, and a zero-to-hero storyline. It also resonated with my audience because it was posted close to the exam period.

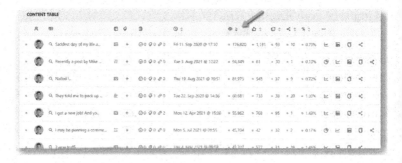

By using Shield app, I was able to reverse engineer why this post worked so well and apply the same principles to my other posts.

I also learned what types of posts didn't work for me, such as how-tos or book summaries, and I stopped posting them.

Advanced analytics are really helpful for you to see what works and what doesn't work for your LinkedIn content. You can use them to double down on what works and eliminate what doesn't. You can also experiment with different types of posts and see how they perform. This way, you can optimize your LinkedIn presence and reach more people with your message.

Establishing your personal brand is a journey of self-discovery and continuous refinement. By taking the time to identify your niche, consistently provide value, and deliberately design your messaging, you can attract ideal opportunities.

Begin by taking stock of your innate strengths, interests, and experiences. Conduct a personal SWOT analysis. How are you uniquely positioned to help others?

Your brand comes into focus when you align your offerings with an underserved market need. Specialize rather than remaining a generalist. Become known as the go-to solution for a tightly defined audience.

Craft a compelling value proposition statement that communicates the tangible outcomes you enable clients to achieve. This provides direction for your branding and content strategies.

Across your website, social media, content, and collateral, ensure complete alignment with your core messaging and personality. Consistency and repetition cement your niche identity.

Measure your effectiveness using tools like LinkedIn's Social Selling Index. Analyse what's working and refine areas needing improvement. Listen to feedback to continually evolve.

Patience is key, as personal brands develop over years, not weeks. But with consistency, your niche focus becomes magnetic. Stay nimble and open to new ways to provide value as you grow.

The road to establishing your reputation requires persistence and humility. But the visibility and authority you build allows serving others on a larger scale.

You now have the blueprint and insights to differentiate yourself in a noisy world. So take the first step to sharing your gifts and making an impact. The journey ahead promises fulfilment if you stay true to your values.

Key Takeaways

- Crafting an effective LinkedIn profile is important for personal branding. A professional photo, optimized headline, and compelling summary that showcases your expertise and value are crucial.
- Thought leadership on LinkedIn can establish you as an industry expert and attract opportunities. Consistently sharing high-quality original content on topics your followers care about through articles and posts helps build influence.
- Your LinkedIn network and connections are an asset to be cultivated and leveraged. Proactively connecting with strategic contacts and engaging in discussions helps nurture meaningful professional relationships.
- Understanding LinkedIn's algorithm and analytics provides insight into what content and strategies are most effective. Consistent posting at optimal times along with engagement can help reach wider audiences.
- Leveraging writing templates streamlines the content creation process for busy entrepreneurs. Established frameworks help generate consistent, high-quality posts without starting from scratch each time.
- Automation tools can help scale key LinkedIn activities while maintaining relevance. Strategic use of tools like

LeadConnect amplifies outreach without sacrificing personalization.

- Advanced analytics reveal in-depth insights beyond the basic metrics LinkedIn provides. Tools like Shield app help benchmark performance and identify factors contributing to top-performing content.

Part III

Launching Your Self-Employment Venture

From Investment Manager to CFO to Consulting Practice: Eric Tan's Inspiring Career Pivot

Like many driven professionals, Eric Tan reached a point where climbing the corporate ladder no longer equalled fulfilment (Tan E., 2023). After years in finance and a stint with a start-up, Eric made the leap in his early thirties to launch his own consultancy.

It was a plunge into the unknown world of entrepreneurship, driven by his lifelong passion for business. Financial security was replaced by uncertainty. Sales and marketing skills had to be built from scratch. His identity shifted from corporate specialist to solopreneur.

Taking a Leap of Faith

Eric started his career in accounting and audit after obtaining his degree, but soon realized his interest lay more in business and entrepreneurship. He explored this by working for a Venture Capital fund investing in start-ups, which further sparked his interest to someday start his own venture.

By his early thirties, Eric knew that if he did not take the risk now, he may never do so as responsibilities increased with age. He decided to take the leap, giving himself one year to meet targets for his consulting business or else return to corporate life.

Eric also started an accounting firm as a separate venture. He had enough savings to cover living expenses for two years without impacting his family's lifestyle, reducing the financial fear factor. His main worry was failure, but he was determined to avoid future regrets by trying.

Bootstrapping the Business

Eric's first venture was a systems integration firm started with a partner to take advantage of an immediate opportunity. After three years, Eric exited this business and pivoted to focus full-time on growing his consultancy, The Resource Group (TRG).

He built TRG up one client at a time leveraging word-of-mouth and referrals. Having competency and expertise in his niche was critical for credible positioning. Eric also gave educational talks and presentations to establish trust as a subject matter expert.

While difficult at first as an introvert, Eric pushed himself to learn sales skills essential for landing clients. He focused on quality and value over competing on price. Today TRG is Eric's primary business, providing 70 per cent of his income. The accounting firm also continues to operate with partners managing day-to-day operations.

Maintaining Work-Life Integration

As his consultancy grew, Eric found his working hours frequently exceeded those in corporate roles. During peak periods, his workweeks stretch to 60–80 hours managing overlapping client deliverables.

But he feels in control by planning projects and schedules strategically. Eric blocks out time for family holidays well in advance, completing deliverables ahead of time and avoiding new work during those periods. While clients sometimes still contact him urgently during time off, he sets boundaries and priorities.

Eric also recognizes and optimizes for his peak productive hours in the afternoons and evenings when handling critical thinking work. He schedules meetings in his less focused mornings. Work-life integration as a business owner remains an ongoing balance.

Key Lessons from Eric's Experience

- **Age doesn't define your potential.** In his early thirties, Eric dared to defy the 'wait and see' mentality, recognizing that delaying his entrepreneurial dream might lead to future regrets.
- **Plan for the jump, but be ready to fly.** Setting a one-year target and having a financial safety net (the accounting firm) allowed Eric to take calculated risks and focus on building his dream.
- **Expert positioning is key.** Eric leveraged his deep understanding of his niche to build credibility and trust, avoiding the trap of competing solely on price.
- **Embrace the salesperson within.** Overcoming his introverted tendencies, Eric honed his sales skills, learning to effectively communicate the benefits of his services.
- **Planning is your superpower.** Eric's strategic scheduling, including pre-booking family vacations

and prioritizing deliverables, helped him stay in control despite demanding work hours.

- **Boundaries are your allies.** Setting clear boundaries with clients during personal time allowed Eric to recharge and prevent burnout.
- **Know your peak times.** Recognizing his most productive hours allowed Eric to schedule critical thinking tasks accordingly, maximizing his efficiency.

Eric Tan's story illustrates how with careful planning and leveraging your strengths, you can pave a path from corporate specialist to thriving solopreneur. Passion and perseverance are keys to finding fulfilment by leading your own professional journey.

Chapter 8

Marketing Your New Venture

'The best marketing doesn't feel like marketing.'
—Tom Fishburne

When I started RecruitPlus back in 2004, marketing was an afterthought compared to just trying to keep the lights on. Print ads and cold calls were my go-to tactics in those early scramble days. Of course, the digital marketing landscape has exploded since then. Over years of experience across recruitment, HR tech, and coaching businesses, I evolved to take a targeted, omnichannel approach based on data and efficacy. Now as a solopreneur, I aim to make every marketing minute count for maximum impact.

In this chapter, I'll break down key lessons on optimizing your marketing strategy as a bootstrapping founder.

As bestselling marketing author Seth Godin puts it, 'Instead of interrupting strangers with ads, great marketers tell stories people want to hear' (Godin, 1999). Effective marketing is not a megaphone shouting about how great you are. It's about crafting compelling stories and providing real value to attract ideal customers who resonate with your message.

This starts with intimately understanding your audience's pain points through customer avatars. Who are their biggest struggles? What keeps them up at night? What outcomes do they desire? With insight into your audience's world, you can position your offerings as the perfect solution.

For instance, Flash Coffee, a tech-enabled coffee chain offering high-quality drinks at competitive prices, identified a market of value-conscious consumers who crave gourmet coffee experiences. This strategic positioning resonated with their target segment, leading to rapid expansion and a loyal customer base. By focusing on convenience and affordability, Flash Coffee successfully challenged the dominance of established players like Starbucks, proving that delicious coffee doesn't have to come at a premium price.

Of course, branding and positioning are just the beginning. You still have to master executing across content, referrals, advertising, and more to turn positioning into profits. This requires diligently tracking metrics to constantly refine and improve performance.

Marketing success ultimately comes down to how compellingly you answer a simple question in your audience's mind: 'Why should I buy from you instead of your competitors?' If your story clearly explains how you understand their struggles better than anyone and offer a uniquely tailored solution, you have cracked their code.

So let's explore proven ways to share persuasive stories that attract perfect customers and enable your purpose. With the right strategy and authentic positioning, your marketing will fuel fulfilling self-employment for years to come!

Developing Your Marketing Strategy

Kicking off any marketing endeavour should begin with crafting a comprehensive marketing strategy. This strategic blueprint will guide your positioning, messaging, channel selection, campaigns, and metrics.

So the first step is intimately understanding your audience's pain points and desires. What frustrates your audience? What are their biggest unmet needs? What outcomes are they seeking?

For example, when I started Marketing Sumo, I identified that HR tech founders struggled with organic lead generation and inbound marketing. They lacked expertise in optimizing platforms like LinkedIn and were overwhelmed trying to balance their inbound efforts with product development and fundraising. This became the 'pain' I aimed to solve.

To truly unlock the hearts and minds of your audience, dive deep into the world of buyer personas. These detailed profiles, built on a foundation of demographic data like job titles, company size, and location, go beyond the surface. They capture your ideal customers' motivations, challenges, values, and even their typical buying journey. Giving your personas names and backstories humanizes them, transforming them from data points into living, breathing individuals you can truly understand and connect with.

Benefits:

- Targeted marketing: Buyer personas inform your marketing efforts, ensuring you speak directly to your ideal customers' needs and desires. No more shouting into the void!
- Enhanced product development: Understanding your audience's pain points and aspirations guides product development, leading to solutions that truly resonate with your target market.
- Boosted sales conversion: By tailoring your sales approach to each persona's buying process and motivations, you'll watch conversion rates soar.
- Improved customer experience: When you understand your audience, you can create personalized experiences that build loyalty and advocacy.

Use Cases:

- Content creation: Craft compelling messaging that resonates with your personas' interests and challenges.
- Social media marketing: Engage your audience with relevant content and targeted advertising.
- Website design and user experience: Build a website that caters to your ideal customers' needs and preferences.
- Product development: Prioritize features and functionalities that address your audience's pain points.

While building detailed buyer personas takes time and effort, tools like Founderpal.ai can offer a helpful shortcut. This AI-powered platform allows you to input your business (e.g., a cold email outreach tool) and target audience segment (e.g., design agency owners) and generate a user persona in seconds. It provides a basic framework, including a description, problem statement, pain points, goals, benefits, and potential triggers and obstacles. Think of it as a springboard for further development. You can then delve deeper into your target audience through market research, interviews, and surveys to flesh out the persona and gain a richer understanding of their motivations and behaviours. Remember, AI tools are valuable for speeding up the process, but human input remains crucial for creating truly insightful buyer personas.

Content Marketing Institute's 2022 B2B Content Marketing Benchmarks, Budgets, and Trends report mentions that 84 per cent of B2B marketers say having documented buyer personas is important for their content marketing strategy (Stahl, 2021).

Clearly defining your ideal customers is crucial.

Defining Your Brand Positioning

Next, use the customer insights to shape your brand positioning and messaging. How will you explain why prospects should buy from or partner with you versus alternatives? What uniquely compelling value do you offer?

For example, I positioned my business as 'B2B marketing services for growth stage founders-led HR Tech.' This immediately communicated specialized expertise for a defined audience.

As a coach and trainer, Adeline Tiah positions her services as 'I equip leaders with the mindset to build sustainable performance and results.' (Tiah, 2023)

This quickly conveys her niche expertise in developing leadership mindsets for improved business outcomes. It speaks directly to her target audience of managers and executives seeking to boost their team's productivity and results in a lasting way.

The key is making your messaging emotional and aspirational. Avoid boring features and specifications. Instead, focus on the outcomes and transformation that your audience desires. Apple didn't say, 'We make computers with cutting-edge components.' They inspired with 'Think Different.' Wrap your offering in an engaging vision that people can connect with at a deeper level.

Craft your positioning around the results you enable clients to achieve, not just the services you provide. Communicate your ability to understand their frustrations and equip them with exactly what they need to overcome those challenges. Distil your competitive difference down to a simple yet compelling message.

I understand it can be enticing to position yourself as broad as possible. Why limit yourself to just a segment when you can get businesses from everywhere?

Firstly, your positioning does not limit you from taking on engagements beyond what you positioned yourself for. For instance, I also do speaking engagements and it isn't something I publicly make mention of. Your positioning should be seen as a preferred type of engagement. You likely won't have a sales team or even the bandwidth to do selling when things get on track. Your funnelling of inbound interests based on your positioning is the next best option to qualify the most ideal future customers.

The other thing is the market can be very competitive. If I simply position my business as Marketing Agency for everybody, I am setting up myself for a race to the bottom and compete with the cheapest alternatives on Fiverr who can price themselves low due to their lower cost base.

At mid-career stage, we can't afford to play the price game. Not with younger competition who can outwork us and especially not with competition from countries with a lower cost of living.

Instead of becoming the #100 in a broad category, I automatically become the #1 in the marketing for just HR Tech vendors category.

And with clarity on positioning, you can consistently reinforce your messaging across channels through stories, content, and campaigns. An authoritative niche focus attracts ideal prospects who resonate with the outcomes you promise to deliver. Keep positioning front and centre as you execute marketing programmes tied back to your strategic foundations.

Setting Marketing Objectives

With your positioning and messaging defined, the next step is outlining specific marketing objectives and key performance indicators (KPIs).

For example, you may set goals to gain ten new clients in six months through content marketing activities. Or target a 15 per cent increase in website traffic driven by Search Engine Optimisation (SEO) efforts.

Having concrete marketing objectives provides several benefits:

- Gives direction: With specific goals established, you can shape strategies, plan campaigns, and allocate resources efficiently to accomplish those aims.
- Enables focus: Well-defined objectives prevent getting distracted by vanity metrics and activities that don't ultimately impact your goals.

- Drives accountability: Putting measurable targets in place creates accountability to execute campaigns that move the needle on those KPIs.
- Allows optimization: Tracking performance against objectives highlights what's working well and what needs refinement. You can double down on high-return activities.
- Provides motivation: Seeing progress towards your marketing goals provides ongoing motivation to keep grinding. Celebrating wins reinforces momentum.

For example, Mel Robbins details her goal of giving 100 speeches in a year (Robbins, 2017). Having this objective guided her speaker submissions and outreach to event organizers.

Entrepreneur and musician Derek Sivers aimed to gain 1,000 email subscribers for his independent music distribution business, CD Baby, within a year. He achieved this by writing engaging content and offering valuable free resources, like a free e-book (Sivers, 2022).

In your own marketing strategy, identify two to three key objectives aligned to your overarching business goals. Outline the specific measurable targets, timeline, and tactics for each. Revisit and adjust quarterly based on results. With clarity on the outcomes that matter most, you can streamline activities to move the needle.

Selecting Marketing Channels

Now that your positioning and objectives are defined, the next step is determining which marketing channels to leverage to reach your audience.

Your options are virtually endless—content marketing, referrals and word-of-mouth, events, advertising, email, social media, direct outreach, and more. It's easy to get overwhelmed by the sea of choices.

The only limitations are your bandwidth and budget. And it is pointless to be stretched so thin to cover all channels that you are left with no time to work on your business.

That's why Seth Godin advocates narrowing your focus to just two or three core channels tailored to your goals and audience. As he puts it, 'Do less better' (Design Better, 2022). Don't get distracted trying to master eight channels. Double down on the ones with the highest pay-off potential for what you offer.

For example, when I decided to write about HR technology, I focused heavily on content marketing through my blog and guest posts. This allowed me to cost-effectively build authority and visibility with my niche audience of HR tech founders. Referrals happened organically as a by-product.

On the other hand, podcast host and entrepreneur Noah Kagan leveraged audio content and partnerships as his core channel mix to establish expertise (Kagan, n.d.). This format aligned with his strengths and offered a differentiated way to reach busy executives always on the go.

Take stock of your own innate abilities and interests. Avoid mimicking others' channels choices without considering fit. Kagan's podcasting genius may fall flat if I tried to copy it. And I am still trying to figure out Instagram, let alone TikTok.

Play to your existing strengths and preferences to determine the best channel mix for you. Across all the subjects I interviewed for this book, 50 per cent of them use LinkedIn as their main distribution channel as that is where their prospects reside.

In many instances, a combination of organic content, referrals, and social media provides sufficient fuel for bootstrapped marketing success. Paid advertising can supplement but is not required initially. I tried paid ads when I first started CareerLadder, my career coaching agency. It did not convert well and I have since shied away from paid ads as a channel.

The ocean contains endless marketing possibilities but chart your course based on what promises the smoothest sailing. Consistency and high-quality execution trumps quantity of channels. Once you gain traction, you can always expand your channel mix. But start with a focused foundation that plays to your strengths.

Crafting Campaigns and Content

The final piece of your marketing strategy is mapping out specific campaigns and content tailored to your positioning, audiences, and channel mix.

For example, when I first established myself in HR Tech, I created an annual market landscape report showcasing all the latest start-ups and innovations in Singapore's HR tech ecosystem.

This provided a free, downloadable asset I could leverage to connect with and build relationships with even more HR tech founders and investors in my target space. It also enabled me to demonstrate domain expertise through sharing insights on trends and growth projections.

Other potential campaigns could include:

- An email nurturing sequence focused on aspiring influencers interested in building their brand and monetizing it.
- A lead magnet guide on 'The 5 Biggest Mistakes People Make on LinkedIn' aimed at professionals wanting to optimize their profile.
- A monthly newsletter with tips, insider perspectives, and resources for new coaches building their practice.
- A video course on actionable strategies for service-based entrepreneurs looking to scale.

The goal is crafting campaigns specifically tailored to your audience avatars and their needs, distributed via your defined channel mix. Great marketing tells compelling stories people want to be part of.

When brainstorming campaigns, tap into your creative strengths. For example, if you are design-savvy and have design expertise, you could consider creating an online course to teach others how to do design. Play to your existing superpowers.

Revisit your campaigns regularly and refine based on performance data. For instance, I evolved my HR tech landscape report into a multi-country study based on feedback. Continual optimization is key.

With strategic clarity on customers, positioning, channels, and campaigns, executing marketing programmes becomes much simpler. You have laid the groundwork for success—now persistently put it into practice.

These strategic foundations allow executing marketing programmes efficiently. Revisit the components regularly as you gain data and feedback. With clarity on customers, messaging and channels, your marketing will propel self-employment success.

Executing Effective Content Marketing

Content marketing has been a crucial component to my current fractional business. Beyond that, my content led me to a role with an India-based enterprise HR tech vendor and my podcast led me to my last employment at the Institute for Human Resources Professionals.

Just like petrol powers a vehicle's engine, high-quality content powers your ability to connect with customers, demonstrate expertise, and drive growth.

As entrepreneur and author Andrew Davis states, 'Content builds relationships. Relationships are built on trust. Trust drives revenue.' (Hallett, 2016)

Consistently publishing valuable content allows you to build relationships, demonstrate expertise, and drive business growth in a cost-effective way.

But determining what content to create and how to promote it can be challenging. This section will explore proven content marketing tactics for the self-employed, including:

- Crafting compelling blog posts that engage your target audience.
- Getting your writing published on other high-authority sites through guest posting.
- Producing quality videos to showcase your knowledge and personality.
- Launching a podcast to build a loyal following in your niche.
- Building an email list and sending regular newsletters packed with insights.
- Optimizing your content for search engines through SEO best practices.

Social media is missing here as that is covered in the previous chapter on personal branding.

By taking a strategic approach to these key content marketing channels, you can establish yourself as a top authority, build meaningful relationships with your audience, and achieve your business goals as a solopreneur.

Crafting Compelling Blog Posts

Blogging can be an extremely effective content marketing channel for establishing yourself as an industry expert and thought leader. However, writing posts that genuinely engage readers takes skill.

For example, my website adriantan.com.sg focuses on human resources technology topics and sharing episodes of my CNA podcast. By consistently publishing quality articles and commentary related to my niche, I've built an audience of over 5,000 monthly visitors today.

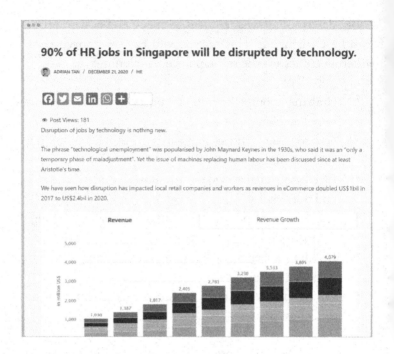

But when launching my blog, writing compelling posts didn't come naturally. Here are some tips I've learned:

- Focus your blog on a specific niche. This allows you to really understand your audience's interests and pain points. At a point in time, I kept digressing and even wrote about parenting stuffs on my blog. That was when traffic started to drop as the site became all over the place. It was when I started to drop non-core genre that the traffic picked up again.
- Outline your posts before writing to organize your thoughts. I often use templates like the SIMPLE framework: Situation, Implication, Problem, Lesson, Example. This provides structure.
- Open with an engaging hook like an intriguing question or timely example. This draws readers in to keep scrolling.

- Use subheads to break up long blocks of text for skimmability. Readers are more likely to stick with your post if it's visually digestible.
- Share personal experiences or examples to connect with readers. But focus on useful takeaways versus just storytelling.
- Link to reputable sources like research reports and expert commentary to back up your assertions. This builds credibility.
- Close with a call to action. Prompt readers to subscribe, share the article, or remember key points. This drives engagement.

Though AI has become a looming presence in the writing industry, I would like to think I have made good use of it to my advantage rather than detriment. One such example is the dictation app Oasis[1]. Forget staring at a blank page, paralyzed by the pressure to craft the perfect sentence. Oasis AI is here to unleash your inner storyteller! Talk freely, let your ideas flow, and watch as Oasis transforms your ramblings into coherent, engaging text. It's like having a personal writing coach in your pocket, guiding you towards clarity and structure without stifling your unique voice. Choose the tone—formal, casual, humorous, or heartfelt—and let Oasis weave your words into a tapestry that reflects your authentic self. Remember, the magic lies in your thoughts and emotions, and Oasis is simply the tool to help them shine brighter.

The key is optimizing for quality rather than chasing quantity. Two superbly crafted niche articles per week will outperform twenty mediocre ones. Stay relentlessly focused on delivering value to your niche audience above all else.

---

[1] https://www.theoasis.com/

Regularly publishing excellent, value-driven blog content is essential for attracting and retaining an audience. But done right, the pay-off in terms of reputation and organic growth can be immense.

Leveraging Guest Posting

In addition to publishing on your own blog, guest posting on reputable third-party publications can significantly expand your reach and credibility. By contributing articles to industry sites, you can tap into new audiences already engaged with those publications.

I've been fortunate to have my writing featured on major sites like Yahoo News, Channel NewsAsia, Lifehacker, The Middle Ground (defunct), and Recruit CRM. This has introduced my personal brand and expertise to wider communities of professionals and tech enthusiasts.

On top of that, I also get backlinks from these reputable sites. This means they will include a hyperlink at the end of my guest post that points to my website. Backlinks will help to improve your site domain authority.

Domain authority refers to a score developed by Moz[2] that predicts how well a website will rank on search engine results pages (SERP). It's one of the key metrics used to measure a site's SEO strength and authority in a particular field.

The domain authority score ranges from 1 to 100, with higher scores indicating greater authority and trust in the eyes of Google and other search engines.

Sites with higher domain authority tend to rank higher and appear more prominently in search results. This leads to increased visibility and website traffic. Google also uses domain authority as one of the factors in determining a site's overall trust and value. Higher authority improves your search real estate.

Linking to sites with higher domain authority passes 'link juice' and improves your own SEO metrics. It boosts perceptions of your credibility.

My usual go-to is Ubersuggest[3] and you can see that my domain authority is at thirty-three.

---

[2] https://moz.com/

[3] https://neilpatel.com/ubersuggest/

A top-rated mainstream news site would carry something significantly higher. For example, Channel NewsAsia has a domain authority at ninety.

Here are some tips for successfully pitching and writing compelling guest posts:

- Identify publications your target audience reads. Focus on reputable sites related to your niche. Build a list of at least ten publications to pitch.
- Thoroughly research each outlet. Understand their content style, tone, and topics. This ensures your pitch and post are a fit.
- Craft a unique angle. Avoid broad themes and aim for posts tailored to that publication's readers. Make the value-add clear.
- Keep your pitch short and specific. Communicate your expertise and article concept in a few concise paragraphs. Make it easy for editors to say yes.
- Co-promote the piece. Once published, announce the post on your own website and social channels. Collaborating expands reach.

- Follow editorial guidelines diligently. Stick to agreed word counts and include links as requested. This ensures a smooth experience for the publisher.

You can also imagine the amount of request that websites or platforms like Channel News Asia may get in a single day asking for permission to guest post or write a commentary. It will take time and a bit of luck to align a trending topic that you may be the most suitable person to contribute about.

Leveraging guest posts allows you to tap into new and engaged audiences while showcasing your expertise. With persistence and compelling pitches, you can secure placements that introduce new readers to your personal brand.

Harnessing the Power of Video

Video content has become a must for modern marketing. According to the Digital 2021 Global Overview Report by Hootsuite and We Are Social, video made up 73 per cent of total internet traffic in 2021, up from 70 per cent in 2020 (We Are Social, Hootsuite, 2021). The report compiles data from hundreds of sources to analyse digital trends. With short attention spans but a voracious appetite for online video, compelling videos can help you connect with and engage your audience.

My own obsession with video began in childhood, glued to the family TV. Later attempts at acting fizzled, but my fascination with the medium persisted. Behind-the-scenes production initially seemed intimidating. However, advancing technology has made quality video much more accessible for everyone.

For example, today's smartphones can capture brilliant 4K footage. With some simple gear and software, cinematic-style videos are within reach. Lighting and post-production still play a role, but the bar has lowered considerably.

I have done my fair share of experimentation of video production and post-production. If you want to achieve modern day YouTube level, it is going to take a long time to achieve that level and to do the editing.

Personally, I will advise against that as the constant tweaking during post production will just delay the actual publication and that in itself will affect the ability to have a regular cadence.

AI tools like Scrip[4] or ChatGPT[5] can be valuable brainstorming partners for video scripts. Use them to generate ideas, explore different angles, and get creative sparks flowing. However, remember to edit and refine the AI-generated content to ensure it aligns with your unique voice and message. Don't let AI dictate your story—use it as a springboard for your own creativity!

Copy the script across to a teleprompter app such as Teleprompter for Video. The script will be displayed near to the front-facing camera so it looks like you are looking at the camera. Keep videos under five minutes whenever possible. People's attention spans are fleeting.

Ready to make your talking head videos shine? Here are the keys to unlock video magic:

- **Light and sound:** Don't underestimate the power of good lighting and audio. A cheap ring light can work wonders, and even basic earphones will improve your sound quality significantly. Remember, viewers prioritize clarity over perfection.

---

[4] https://scripai.com/

[5] https://chat.openai.com/

- **Effortless engagement:** Want to take your videos to the next level? Tools like Submagic can be your secret weapon. This awesome platform seamlessly generates captions with relevant emojis and keyword highlights, adding visual interest and accessibility to your content. It's a game-changer for busy creators who want to elevate their videos without sacrificing time or energy.

- **Fun is key:** Remember, creating videos should be enjoyable. Don't get bogged down in technicalities. Have fun with it, experiment, and let your unique voice come through. Video might require more effort than writing, but the impact it has on your audience is undeniable. With a little practise and the right tools, you can add this powerful medium to your marketing mix and watch your engagement soar.

Podcasting to Expand Your Reach

Podcasting continues to grow as an influential content marketing channel. There are limited concrete data available on podcast statistics specifically for Southeast Asian countries. But if we look at what is available, Statista projects the global number of podcasts to reach 4.4 million by 2027 (Statista, n.d.).

As the host of *The Adrian Tan Show* and co-host of *Work It* by CNA, I've seen first-hand how podcasts can expand your personal brand and thought leadership.

It can even lead to opportunities. As I shared, my own podcast led me to my previous employment. Around that time, I was looking out for new opportunities and shared that with all my guests and one of them happens to be my former boss who said there may be something and the rest is history.

The experience in doing my own podcast also made me a consideration for CNA when they were looking to start a work-related podcast. It is also a contributing reason to my current assignment with the SAP SuccessFactors implementation partners as one of my scopes is to host their business podcast.

One good thing I found about podcasting is you have another reason to reach out to prospects beyond just a sales pitch. Ask ten people to buy from you, nine may slam the door. But ask them if they want to guest on your podcast, I'm confident at least half will say yes.

Back when I first dipped my toes into the podcasting waters, the experience was a far cry from today's streamlined reality. Post-production was a costly ordeal, and our audio quality suffered due to inadequate equipment. Five episodes in, the hurdles proved too much, and I had to pull the plug. But fast forward to the present, and the landscape has shifted dramatically. Post-production is now as effortless as editing text, and with the magic of modern tools, even basic audio can be elevated to studio quality. This democratization of podcasting has removed the barriers to entry, making it an accessible and powerful tool for anyone to connect with their target audience.

If you are looking to explore podcasting, here are some tips:

- **Choose a tight niche:** This gives you focus and helps attract a targeted audience interested in that specific topic. If you already have picked a business niche, your podcast should be similar or adjacent to that niche so that it complements.
- **Equipment:** I would recommend a USB condenser mic and a good webcam if you are doing video. Don't bother with a mixer. That is too much.
- **Interview style:** Interviewing others is an easy format and showcases your network. And most of the airtime will be filled by your guest. All you need to ensure is an expressive guest and great questions.

- **Virtual studio:** Using a platform like SquadCast[6], you can have your own recording studio virtually. The difference between them versus using Zoom is these dedicated platforms tend to record in higher quality and each speaker is recorded separately. This mean if there are intermittent internet issues, the recording will not be affected. If you are doing a video podcast, separate tracks will make it easier for many editing tools to bring speakers to view depending on who is talking.

- **Postproduction:** I wasn't kidding when I said postproduction is as easy as editing text. A tool like Descript[7] will transcript your audio and the track can be adjusted when you edit the text. It can even detect filler words such as ummms and remove them automatically. Lastly it has a Studio Sound feature that turns your audio to studio quality.

- **Hosting:** You need a place to house your podcast on the internet and Spotify for Podcasters[8] is a great place to start. And it is free.

Starting and sustaining a podcast requires effort but can pay dividends in establishing your reputation and expertise. These can lead to new opportunities and even the possibility of monetizing your episodes as I managed to for a few of mine.

Building Your Email List

Email marketing remains one of the most effective ways to engage your audience. I've built my own email list to include over

---

[6] https://squadcast.fm/

[7] https://www.descript.com/

[8] https://podcasters.spotify.com/

1.1K subscribers and grown my LinkedIn newsletter list to 14K followers. Email provides a direct channel to nurture relationships, unaffected by unpredictable social media algorithms.

My personal approach now is to send a weekly newsletter that summarizes my key thought, highlights podcast episodes, and shares useful resources related to my niche. That could be in the form of a tool, an interesting video I came across, or a great book I just completed.

Just like many other channels, starting a newsletter today is easier than ever. In fact, it has been made really easy with the likes of Mailchimp[9] and MailerLite[10] (I personally use this). There are newer ones such as beehiiv[11] that has made the entire process even simpler.

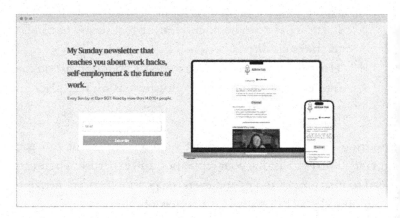

If you are starting out, the tool does not matter much. It is the regularity of the unique content you will be sharing that is more important. My newsletter goes out every Sunday unless I am away on a holiday.

---

[9] https://mailchimp.com/

[10] https://www.mailerlite.com/

[11] https://www.beehiiv.com/

And if you are new, you want to give incentive to your audience for exchanging their email addresses for your content. This can be done by offering a freebie such as a guide, checklist, or template.

For example, CEO Coach Eric Partaker provides a free pdf copy of his book *The 3 Alarms* to encourage his audience to sign up for his newsletter (Partaker, 2020). Personally, I have a Productivity Tools Guide that I give out as a pdf to entice my audience to become subscribers.

Despite what is said, email is not dead, and it shall remain one of the best tools for sharing your knowledge and nurturing relationships.

Speaking Opportunities to Showcase Expertise

Securing speaking engagements is a powerful way to establish credibility and grow your personal brand as an industry expert.

I actively pursue relevant conference and corporate speaking opportunities. For example, I've delivered keynotes on topics like future of work at HR tech events, universities, and companies.

It wasn't an easy start for me as I do get massive stage fright. My first speaking engagement was also a flop where it ended with a fraction of the number of people who started.

Jerry Seinfeld mentioned in one of his stand-ups that people's number two fear is death. And their number one fear is public speaking. So between laying down in the coffin and delivering the eulogy, people would choose the former!

But seriously, public speaking isn't just about bragging rights. There's real merit to the skills it builds.

Take Ratna Juita for instance. To help accelerate her speaking skills, she joined Toastmaster to gain the necessary skills and sparring practice to improve herself (Juita, 2023).

Practice need not only come from joining a community. Steve Jobs practised his keynote in front of a mirror multiple times before the actual delivery (Isaacson, 2011). Content creator Jeraldine Phneah[12] does the same to hone her sales pitch.

For me, it was just the reps that I continue to put in whether it was a TV interview or another speaking event. (I apologize to all my earlier audience who acted as my mirror for me to improve and be where I am today.)

If this is an arena you are keen to consider, start mapping out the event organizer you should be building relationships with. Given my niche, it would be companies such as HRM Asia, *HumanResources*, and People Matters.

For your first few speaking engagements, it likely would be paid with publicity. That is usually the case as you may not have the track record to show your speaking prowess. Use the opportunity to gain footage and testimonials that will equip you better to secure future paid gigs.

It would be wise to create a speaker one-sheet that would include everything about you as a speaker. This can be done on a Google Doc and you can easily update the master copy and distribute it electronically.

The sheet would include:

- Headshot
- Biography – The bio should be short, about three to five concise sentences focused on your credentials and achievements related to your speaking niche.
- Niche/Expertise – Summarize your relevant experience and qualifications in one to two sentences. This highlights why you're worth hearing from.
- Speech Topics – Include the title of each speech you offer along with a two to three sentence description summarizing the focus.

---

[12] https://www.jeraldinephneah.com/

- Takeaways/Benefits – Briefly list three to five key benefits the audience will gain from your presentation. These should connect to their goals and interests.

- Past Engagements – Provide three to five highlights of past speaking gigs to showcase your experience. Name the event and your role.

- Testimonials – Provide one to two brief testimonials that validate your abilities as a speaker. Include the name, title, and company of the person quoted.

- Contact Details – List your email address and phone number so event planners can easily reach out.

Launching your own venture is exhilarating, but effective marketing is essential for visibility and long-term viability. With strategic foundations and savvy execution, you can fuel sustainable self-employment through your marketing.

Start with intimate understanding of your ideal customer through detailed personas. Map their pain points and desires. Then position your offerings as the perfect solution.

Select a focused channel mix that aligns with your strengths, resources, and audience. Depth trumps breadth. Avoid spreading efforts too thin.

Create campaigns and content specifically tailored to your personas and channels. Focus on quality and relevance over vanity metrics.

Measure performance rigorously and double down on high-ROI activities. Continually refine based on data and feedback.

Stay nimble—experiment with new channels and campaigns, but cull ones that don't gain traction after testing.

Your marketing strategy must answer one key question: Why you over competitors? Tell compelling stories that make your solution irresistible.

With the right customer insights, positioning, and strategies, your marketing will propel your business forward. Remain grounded in impact, not noise.

You now have the blueprint for sharing your purpose and gifts at scale. So take the leap to connect with those needing exactly what you offer. Start putting it into practice! With focus and persistence, your marketing will fuel the freedom to do meaningful work that matters.

Key Takeaways

- A comprehensive marketing strategy helps you define your target audience, brand positioning, value proposition, objectives, and channels.
- Buyer personas and business positioning help you communicate the valuable outcomes you enable for your customers and their pain points.
- Marketing channels and campaigns help you execute your strategy and reach your customers using various formats and tactics.
- Content marketing and thought leadership help you build your expertise, visibility, and relationships with your audience and industry peers.
- Performance tracking and refinement help you optimize your results and achieve your objectives using data and feedback.

Chapter 9

Assembling Your Dream Team: Building Your Self-Employment Support Network

'Alone we can do so little; together we can do so much.'
—Helen Keller

The isolation I felt when I first started my solo career coaching business after exiting my recruitment agency was palpable. Having spent over a decade leading a team of thirty employees in a bustling office environment, I suddenly found myself working solo from a small desk in my quiet dining room.

Gone were the days of lively banter with colleagues that made the hours fly by. Instead, I faced long days of silence, without even a phone ringing or the clatter of keyboards to disrupt the monotony. The deafening quiet while I worked alone on backend tasks like building my website was jarring.

I missed having teammates to connect with. Without an entrepreneurial support network yet, I often felt like I was navigating uncharted waters alone, without a compass or map to guide me. The solitude challenged me far more than I expected as an extrovert who thrived off the buzz of vibrant workplaces.

I yearned for those informal watercooler chats where entrepreneurial peers could swap stories, wins, and lessons learned. I craved the laughter, encouragement, and sense of belonging that came from being part of a community. The isolation made the typical start-up struggles with cashflow, client acquisition, and managing overhead feel exponentially harder.

Having always worked in traditional corporate structures before, I lacked understanding of how invaluable a support squad is for sustaining motivation, gaining guidance, and building resilience as a solopreneur. My inner world was dimmer without the sparks of human connection.

In hindsight, I wished I had proactively focused on assembling my own 'dream team' of mentors, collaborators, and mastermind network in those early days of my business. Having fellow travellers along the journey would have eased the rocky road. If I could redo that chapter, I would have invested significant time nurturing relationships and my community simultaneously as I built my business.

In this chapter, I aim to help you avoid the needless isolation I experienced by equipping you to proactively build their community and support systems early on.

The Immense Value of Having a Strong Support Network

Taking the first steps down the solopreneur path can feel like wandering into an uncharted forest alone, with no trail or signs to guide you. The terrain ahead is veiled in uncertainty. Self-doubt and isolation lurk behind every bend along the way. With no fellow travellers or map, it's all too easy to lose your bearings when the journey gets rocky.

This is precisely why cultivating a strong support network is absolutely vital for any aspiring solopreneur. Your community acts as both compass and lantern, illuminating your path ahead while keeping you oriented in the right direction. They grant you the courage and resilience to continue putting one foot in front of the other, even when the road gets steep or you face unexpected obstacles.

In many ways, your network is your net worth as an entrepreneur. The meaningful relationships you nurture uplift and sustain you during the low moments every founder inevitably faces. They open doors to pivotal opportunities that can accelerate your progress tremendously. Your comrades along the journey bring camaraderie that makes the adventure far more enjoyable, and weaves in unforgettable memories.

There are several forms of invaluable support on the solopreneur path:

- **Mentors:** Those who have walked the trail ahead of you can provide guidance, insights, and advice to help you sidestep common pratfalls that may lie in wait. Their hard-earned experience grants you a shortcut to the wisdom it took them years or even decades to accumulate through trial and error, saving you precious time and avoidable pain.
- **Peers:** Fellow solopreneurs on parallel journeys can intimately relate to your day-to-day realities. They offer empathy, encouragement, and highly practical tips shaped by their own recent learning. Shared stories of small wins and major milestones help fuel your motivation during difficult stretches.
- **Groups:** Entrepreneurial mastermind communities create a space for networking, collaborating, and exchanging ideas. The spark of human connection provides inspiration and accountability to turn your visions into reality.

Let's explore the specific value of each of these support pillars in greater depth:

Mentors – Your Yoda and Obi Wan

We all need our own personal Yoda or Obi Wan Kenobi—those sagely mentors who guide us in harnessing our potential. Their beads of wisdom gained from walking the path ahead steer us towards growth and achievement.

For solopreneurs, mentors provide invaluable direction in navigating the often-murky waters of building a business. They can illuminate blind spots from their aerial vantage point, helping you anticipate unseen currents or obstacles downstream. Their past failures witnessed first-hand grant you insider tips to avoid similar fates.

By sharing proven frameworks, models, and resources that enabled their own success, mentors allow you to stand on their broad shoulders rather than reinventing the wheel. The years of experience they grant you helps compress decades of learning into mere months or weeks. Their networks built over time can unlock doors that you may spend years trying to open otherwise.

While nearing the summit of entrepreneurial actualization, remember to glance back occasionally towards the mentors who put you on the ascent path. Their wisdom lays the foundation for your success.

How do you find your mentors?

Before that, let me bring you back to 2008, the fourth year since I co-founded RecruitPlus. Just a few months ago, we received an email enquiry about a potential acquisition from another recruitment agency. They focus on marketing recruitment but are looking to acquire new agencies to support a new sister brand that will focus on Office Support recruitment.

After meeting up with the local and regional country manager, we went into due diligence.

As part of the process, the global CEO dropped by Singapore and checked out our operations. We were introduced to Greg Savage, a genteel Australian gentleman who was CEO of their substantial global recruitment firm headquartered in Melbourne. Greg handed me his business card, which felt heavyweight and expensive. Everything about them exuded success and sophistication, especially contrasted against our decidedly bare bones operation.

Greg and I in particular hit it off swimmingly. His achievements were legendary within the recruitment world, having founded and profitably exited from numerous ventures across geographies from Australia to the UK.

Though he was a grizzled industry veteran before I was even born, Greg had an affable, approachable air about him. His eyes twinkled with zest for life and entrepreneurship. He offered us eager young founders valuable perspective from having walked many miles down the path we were just beginning to tread.

Following that momentous first meeting, Greg invited us out to continue conversations over lunch at a quaint restaurant nearby. Between bites, he started inquiring about my personal backstory and how I ended up here.

'You had zero experience running any kind of business before starting this agency. How on earth did you manage to figure everything out along the way?' he asked, with a mix of intrigue and awe.

Partly tongue-in-cheek, I told him—'Google.'

He smiled and replied, 'Google cannot teach you how to get out of a recession.'

While Greg's company ended up not acquiring ours, I vividly recall feeling we were on the cusp of something momentous during our brief time crossing paths.

And he was spot on. When the global financial crisis hit Singapore, Google did not give me a good answer.

Its devasting ripple effects decimated recruitment agencies across Singapore overnight when companies froze hiring en masse.

As this tidal wave of economic calamity crashed down, I sombrely reflected on our providential meeting with Greg back in 2004. I keenly wished I had taken the initiative following that encounter to nurture Greg as a trusted adviser given his decades of experience navigating market downturns.

His hard-won wisdom could have proven invaluable, like a lighthouse guiding our fragile vessel around these treacherous unknown waters.

Instead, my naive impulses at the time were ruled solely by panic and misguided intuition. I pridefully burned through our modest cash reserves trying to keep our fledgling operation afloat, despite the market itself capsizing around us. But these desperate machinations achieved little beyond delaying the inevitable. In hindsight, resisting the prevailing economic winds only damaged our small craft further.

This baptism by fire seared deeply the potentially lifesaving value an experienced mentor could have offered our foundering start-up in those darkest hours. Their mastery of situations and obstacles you have not yet encountered can spur you down the optimal path when confronted with pivotal crossroads. Mentors light the way forward by illuminating stretches ahead they themselves have conquered before you. An adept mentor provides a compass to keep your entrepreneurial bearings straight regardless of which way the winds may shift.

From that formative experience, I vowed to proactively seek out and cultivate meaningful mentoring relationships during every subsequent entrepreneurial endeavour of mine. This conviction drove me to connect with people who have been there, done that as informal advisers during both my niche consultancy and specialized coaching agency years later.

So how do you go about finding your first mentor? Unfortunately there isn't an easy answer. A good start though is to establish a clear goal. What exactly are you trying to achieve? This will help point you in the right direction. If you are trying to set up a drop shipping business, you likely won't want to start with the mentor who achieved success in the brick-and-mortar business. By knowing what your goals are, it will help you narrow down and identify the type of mentor you need and what you can expect from them.

With that, you can then do your research and look for people who have that set of skills, experience, and values that you admire and want to emulate. With the prevalence of LinkedIn, research has gotten much easier with a few keystrokes and clicks. But not all mentors might be active on LinkedIn. One of my friend and mentor Steven Seek is not a LinkedIn regular. Steven was the MD for JobsDB for a decade, and at one point, it wasn't even reflected on his LinkedIn (Seek, n.d.). Such gems are discovered when you know enough people and I was fortunate to know him in a different capacity when I was a client of JobsDB.

Asking fellow self-employed who are on the same or similar path may also help you uncover some folks you might not have otherwise heard of or identify online.

I have found and ascertained that approaching such conversation from an advice angle almost always work. Psychologically people enjoy giving advice. And in certain instance, if they see so much of themselves in you, helping you is almost like helping themselves when they were younger and struggling alone. Explain why you are reaching out and why you are interested to learn from them. Be polite and respectful of their time and availability.

Once you're ready to reach out to someone, it's important to keep things casual. Your approach to a potential mentor should be the same as it would be to a potential friend—your relationship will develop over time. Don't force things; stay relaxed. Lessons and advice will come with time.

Once you've met with a promising mentor and had an initial conversation, think carefully about how and when to follow up. If they're open to continuing a dialogue, set yourself calendar reminders to follow up and set up meetings. How often you speak with your mentor is up to you, but the goal is continued long-term insight. That could mean hopping on the phone or meeting for coffee once a quarter or even twice a year.

Mentors may not have all the answers that you seek but there will always be wisdom that could be imparted across to make your self-employment journey much easier.

The Power of Peer Groups

When traversing the often-lonely solopreneur path filled with twists and turns, connecting with fellow entrepreneurs who've walked similar ground can provide incredible camaraderie, motivation, and strength to persevere during the challenging times.

I experienced the power of peer support first-hand back in 2015 after exiting my first major business venture. During that difficult transitional period ridden with self-doubt and uncertainty about my future path, serendipity led me to a local event called 'Fuckup Nights'. This raw, authentic gathering brought together entrepreneurs and founders to openly share lessons and mistakes learned from their failures in an unfiltered way.

That courageous vulnerability resonated deeply with me, making me feel less alone in my own struggles and self-criticism. I realized that only fellow entrepreneurs could truly relate to the emotional rollercoaster ride every founder endures. Hearing their stories of overcoming major stumbles and continuing to pick themselves back up gave me hope and illuminated a path forward. If they could recover and evolve after major failures, so could I. Motivated by this sense of solidarity and possibility from connecting with peers, I gathered my courage and volunteered to speak at their next event to share my own humbling start-up failures and lessons learned the hard way (Engineers.SG, 2015). That experience cemented for me the immense power of peer empowerment on an entrepreneurial journey often marked by solitary grind and quiet despair.

Over the subsequent years, I've intentionally focused on forming meaningful relationships and bonds with fellow solopreneurs and founders that have organically blossomed into enduring friendships way beyond surface-level business collaborations. While I haven't joined any formal mastermind groups, cultivating these one-on-one peer connections based on our shared entrepreneurial paths has been hugely inspirational, educational, and fulfilling.

For example, The Resource Group's Eric Tan generously opened up about how he structured the financials and cash flow for his consultancy agency in order to maximize stability and profitability based on his naturally prudent and risk-averse personality. His candid advice and framework on balancing profit goals versus chasing short-term revenue growth had a profound impact on shaping how I intentionally ran my own agency to focus on sustainability.

Through conversations with Mumpreneur Nancy Lai, I realized that building a successful long-term business requires persevering through the grind without compromising on sustainable profitability or getting seduced by quick gains or shortcuts. Her insights provided me invaluable reality checks whenever I faced tempting options that seemed too good to be true. Nancy helped reinforce that real, lasting success comes from playing the long game.

At its core, establishing meaningful peer connections and relationships taps into our innate human need for community, shared experiences, and belonging. Fellow entrepreneurs inherently understand the realities, stresses, and responsibilities you face each day because they have walked in your shoes. They can relate to the rollercoaster of emotions, uncertainties, and sacrifices that come with building something from the ground up.

Your peers can spot challenges or blind spots you might miss because you are heads-down just pushing ahead day-to-day. Their eyes light up with genuine excitement and recognition when you achieve a hard-won milestone because they truly know the long journey and relentless effort it required to reach that destination. In essence, your fellow entrepreneurs who understand the path provide hard-to-find context, empathy, and encouragement during the long days when you feel like you are struggling through the wilderness alone. Your peers are comrades who can provide hard-earned strength, wisdom, and hope gleaned from their own miles travelled to urge you on.

Tips for Finding and Building Your Community of Peer Entrepreneurs

While formal mastermind groups provide organized support, equally valuable connections can form organically if you are proactive.

Leverage platforms like Meetup.com to discover relevant events and groups in your area. For example, the Toastmasters Club of Singapore hosts a monthly TMCS Entrepreneur Club focused on helping entrepreneurs grow through networking and idea sharing (Toastmasters Club of Singapore, n.d.).

Their events feature guest speakers, workshops, and networking opportunities with other like-minded founders and peers. Attending Meetups like this can help expand your community.

As decorated military veteran and philanthropist Steve Maraboli wisely stated, 'If you hang out with chickens, you're going to cluck. If you hang out with eagles, you will soar' (Maraboli, 2013). The same principle applies to carefully curating your entrepreneurial peer group—surround yourself with people exhibiting the qualities and mindsets you aim to embrace.

Outsourcing and Delegation: Leveraging External Help to Scale Your Business

It's tempting to try and handle everything yourself. But delegating tasks allows you to focus your time and energy on the highest-value activities that leverage your unique strengths. As Richard Branson wisely stated, 'If you want to grow, learn to delegate.' (Clarkson, 2015)

Here are some of the key benefits of outsourcing and delegation for solopreneurs:

- Frees up your time and mental bandwidth to focus on high-value tasks better suited to your strengths and genius zone. Outsourcing repetitive or specialized work allows you to spend more time on strategy, innovation, and vision.
- Allows you to scale your business capabilities and bandwidth beyond what you can handle personally as an individual. Having an on-demand team via outsourcing provides leverage to grow your business.
- Gain access to specialized expertise and skills you may lack as a solopreneur. For example, leveraging freelance designers, developers, writers, researchers, virtual assistants, and outsourced business development reps.
- Increased speed and efficiency of task execution, since outsourced providers can have more dedicated time and focus on particular tasks they specialize in.
- Tap into fresh perspectives, ideas, and insights from others to augment your thinking. Outsiders can bring new approaches.
- Reduces stress and administrative workload by offloading tasks that are a cognitive drain or distraction from priorities. Achieve better work-life blend.
- Allows you to take advantage of time zone differences by delegating work during your off-hours. For example, outsourcing customer service overnight.
- Cost savings in some cases—specialized freelancers, virtual assistants, and automation tools can be more affordable than hiring full-time staff.

- Added flexibility and scalability to grow or retract your support team as business needs change, since outsourced help is available on-demand.

When order volumes for my first published book unexpectedly skyrocketed, I enlisted my three enthusiastic helpers, my kids, aged between six and ten. It wasn't just about getting things shipped; it was a fun family bonding activity where we worked together, learned about running a small business, and celebrated each completed order with high fives. Sure, there were moments of spilled tape and misplaced stickers, but those were quickly overshadowed by the shared accomplishment and genuine laughter that filled our evenings. While not replicable for all, this demonstrated the power of delegating repetitive tasks.

Sharing Knowledge, Scaling Impact: How I Partner with Student Interns

Leveraging student interns for free support can be a win-win situation. Platforms like Next Step Connections and InternsGoPro make it easy to connect with eager minds from diverse backgrounds, while simultaneously empowering yourself to scale your projects and impact. Over the years, I've hosted over ten international interns, partnering with them in research, content development, and administrative tasks.

My work heavily relied on content creation, where interns played a crucial role in research, outlining, and even drafting initial pieces. This allowed me to shift my focus towards editing and polishing their work, ultimately scaling my output and reaching a wider audience.

However, the benefits extended beyond my own productivity. Each intern brought a unique perspective and fresh ideas to the table, enriching the content and offering alternative viewpoints.

Witnessing their intellectual growth and development as they tackled new challenges was incredibly rewarding.

Working with interns, especially those new to the professional world, requires thoughtful guidance and mentorship. Breaking down tasks into smaller, manageable steps ensured they felt equipped and confident. While there were instances where initial drafts required revision, these moments became opportunities for collaborative learning and refinement.

Tap Agencies to Add Team Bandwidth

Another source of support you can tap into would be suppliers who might be able to scale and do a better job of ancillary work faster. For instance, when I first started my podcast back in 2016, editing was just unfathomable for me. Hence we sent the file to a podcast editor and paid US$50 per episode.

When I was overwhelmed with assignments during the initial phase of my self-employment journey, I also engaged external writers to help me in creating content. One of them is Express Writers[1]. They operate somewhat like an agency and will connect you with the writers most suitable depending on your scope.

For more in-depth and localized content, I went with a Singapore-based content agency With Content[2]. They specialize in B2B tech content and were instrumental in supporting me with my deliverables when it was too overwhelming for me. That came in the form of blog posts and whitepapers, which are thoroughly researched and well-written.

Content may not be a scope of service for all of you. Which brings me to the most common tasks to outsource for many, and that is administration or one-off setup.

---

[1] https://expresswriters.com/

[2] https://withcontent.co/

Via Fiverr[3] or Upwork[4], you can easily put down your job scope and wait for the right bidders that fit your budget. Or you can scroll through the list of talents that are available and find the one that may make most sense for you.

I had engaged talents on these platforms to clean up my website, do site migrations, and even to help me in researching HR tech companies when I was commissioned to develop HR Tech Market Maps for Thailand, Hong Kong, Japan, and Australia as I wasn't familiar with those markets.

Any form of tasks can be outsourced and it should be centred around tasks that can be done adequately by anyone else and will free up time for you to do strategic work that no one else is better equipped to do.

Although your outsourced talents would be more experienced than interns, it is still important to provide them with instructions that are crystal clear. This is especially if it is a design requisition. Designers will rarely ensure your artwork will be their next masterpiece. They just want to get through it as fast as possible because they are likely compensated on deliverables and not time spent.

You should provide your Virtual Assistant with detailed and specific instructions on how to handle each task, including the desired outcome, the deadline, the format, and the resources. You can use screenshots, videos, or templates to illustrate your instructions. Tools like Loom[5] and Guidde[6] can help you record your instructions with your webcam and on your monitor.

---

[3] https://www.fiverr.com/

[4] https://www.upwork.com/

[5] https://www.loom.com/

[6] https://www.guidde.com/

AI as a Partner, Not a Replacement

The rise of AI tools like ChatGPT and Claude offers intriguing possibilities for solopreneurs. Imagine a virtual assistant capable of research, drafting, and even optimization—it sounds like a dream, right? But before we jump on the AI bandwagon, let's talk about a balanced perspective.

Yes, there's a stigma surrounding AI-generated content. Questions of originality, ethics, and dependence linger. I get it. I wouldn't be here using these tools if I wasn't acutely aware of these concerns.

So, how do I leverage AI without falling prey to the pitfalls? The key is intentionality and boundaries. These tools aren't meant to generate the final, polished masterpiece you share with the world. They're partners in specific, well-defined tasks.

Here's how I've used AI tools like ChatGPT:

- Research assistant: AI tackles initial research, pulling together information on a set topic. But the fact-checking and analysis remain firmly in my hands.
- Drafting support: For repetitive tasks like FAQs or market reports, AI provides a starting point. I then refine and personalize the content with my unique voice and expertise.
- Content optimization: AI can suggest keywords and phrasing tweaks to improve page searchability, but the final copy always reflects my brand and message.

Take my services website. I defined target customer personas and specific goals for each page. Then, I provided ChatGPT with competitor examples I liked and asked it to draft new content aligned with those parameters. The AI produced a strong starting point, which I tailored and revised to perfect my voice and message.

The magic lies in understanding where AI shines: bounded tasks, repetitive work, and initial data gathering. For anything requiring creativity, critical thinking, or brand authenticity, human expertise remains irreplaceable.

If you're a solopreneur juggling multiple hats, AI tools can be valuable time-savers. But approach them with caution, with clear boundaries and expectations. Remember, they're partners, not replacements. Use them strategically, stay conscious of potential downsides, and never lose sight of your unique voice and expertise.

Ready to experiment? Try this prompt: 'I need a research assistant to gather key insights on [topic] from reliable sources. Compile a two-page summary with bullet points and citations, focusing on [specific aspects].'

Remember, AI is a powerful tool, but just like any tool, it's how we wield it that truly matters. By approaching it with intentionality and focus, we can unlock its potential while safeguarding our creativity, authenticity, and ultimately, the human edge that makes our solopreneur ventures truly unique.

Mastering the Art of Delegation

We've explored the immense potential of delegation—freeing yourself from micromanagement and unlocking the talents of your team. But effective delegation takes more than just assigning tasks. It requires cultivating a collaborative environment built on clear expectations, trust, and mutual support. That's where these essential tips come into play, designed to guide you towards fostering a culture of empowered delegation within your team.

Now, let's delve into the practical steps to ensure successful delegation:

- Provide detailed instructions on expected outcome, quality standards, deadlines, and format. It all starts with a solid foundation. Before handing off the reins, invest time in providing crystal-clear instructions. Outline the desired outcome, set quality standards, establish deadlines, and define the preferred format. Leave no room for ambiguity; the clearer your expectations, the smoother the execution.

- Set clear expectations on communication protocols and availability requirements. Start small. Instead of throwing your team into the deep end with high-stakes projects, begin with bite-sized tasks. This allows you to provide constructive feedback, identify potential challenges, and gradually build trust in their abilities. As they master smaller tasks, delegate increasingly complex ones, fostering a sense of accomplishment and growth.

- Invest time training delegates early and have them demonstrate capabilities. Don't just assign tasks—invest in your team's growth. Dedicate time to training delegates early on, equipping them with the necessary skills and knowledge to excel. Have them demonstrate their capabilities before diving into complex projects, building their confidence and ensuring successful outcomes.

- Start small with bite-sized tasks before assigning business-critical projects. Instead of throwing your team into the deep end with high-stakes projects, begin with bite-sized tasks. This allows you to provide constructive feedback, identify potential challenges, and gradually build trust in their abilities. As they master smaller tasks, delegate increasingly complex ones, fostering a sense of accomplishment and growth.

- Maintain oversight with periodic status updates and spot checks on work. Delegation doesn't mean relinquishing control. Maintain periodic oversight through regular status updates and spot checks on work. This allows you to provide timely feedback, ensure quality standards are met, and offer support when needed. Remember, your guidance and oversight are crucial for keeping projects on track.

- Show appreciation to delegates who consistently deliver quality work on time. Finally, don't forget the power of appreciation. Acknowledge and celebrate the outstanding work of your team. Showing genuine appreciation reinforces positive behaviour, motivates your team, and strengthens the foundation of trust and collaboration essential for successful delegation.

By incorporating these tips, you can transform delegation from a managerial headache to a powerful tool for boosting your team's productivity, unlocking their hidden talents, and empowering them to thrive. Remember, delegation is a shared journey—trust your team, provide them with the necessary support, and watch as they rise to the challenge, propelling your team and your goals to new heights.

The self-employment journey can feel desolate without camaraderie. But you needn't traverse this path alone. Actively building your support squad surrounds you with uplifting community.

Seek out mentors whose seasoned guidance illuminates pitfalls ahead. Connect with peers who intimately relate to your day-to-day realities. Join masterminds that spark accountability.

Be proactive in nurturing these relationships—they won't form through passive waiting. Ask how you can help mentors before requesting advice. Show up consistently for peers.

Schedule regular check-ins and meetings to sustain your support circle. Use tools like email newsletters and video calls to stay connected in between.

Outsource tasks misaligned with your zone of genius to reliable freelancers and virtual assistants. Automate administrative work using systems and tools. Delegate to scale your impact.

You need not embark on your venture alone. With consistent effort, curate a personal 'board of directors' who believe in your mission and rally around your wins and struggles.

By investing in meaningful relationships, you assemble a dream team that provides strength, wisdom, and community needed to thrive.

Key Takeaways

- **Build Your Dream Team:** Surround yourself with experienced mentors, peer networks, and mastermind groups for guidance, empathy, and practical insights. Seek regular check-ins and authentic one-on-one connections for enduring support and accountability.
- **Outsource Strategically:** Free up your time and leverage expertise by delegating non-essential tasks to freelancers or your team. Provide clear instructions, train effectively, and show appreciation to empower your collaborators.
- **Embrace Technology:** Utilize AI tools as research assistants or for initial drafts, but ensure your unique voice and expertise remain at the forefront.
- **Prioritize Connection:** Maintain regular communication and check-ins across your support system to nurture meaningful relationships over time. Invest in these connections and assemble your dream team of wisdom, strength, and community to thrive as a solopreneur.
- **Seek Constant Growth:** Actively seek out mentorship from relevant industry experts, participate in events and groups, and consider platforms like Meetup.com to discover local communities for continuous learning and inspiration.

From Corporate Marketer to Solopreneur Coach: How Adeline Tiah Took Charge of Her Career

We often romanticize the idea of quitting our jobs to pursue our passions. But leaving the stability of a corporate career for self-employment can be daunting (Tiah, Interview, 2023).

That was the challenge facing Adeline, a seasoned marketer who had risen up the ranks in major companies over twenty years. Yet in her forties, Adeline could feel a career crossroad approaching. She yearned to find more meaning by making a larger impact.

An illuminating workshop sparked the seed several years prior. But it was the disruption of COVID-19 that watered it into fruition. Writing a book on the future of work finally gave Adeline the push to take the leap into self-employment as a career coach.

Embracing Discomfort as a Stepping Stone

For Adeline, the transition to becoming a solopreneur was an incremental, iterative process. She had first taken a career break seven years ago to spend time coaching professionals seeking jobs.

Her experiences revealed how ill-prepared many corporate professionals were for the future economy. It planted the idea that perhaps one day, Adeline could equip people with those missing skills.

When Adeline eventually returned to corporate life, she joined a start-up. Here, she expanded her skills in areas like design thinking and agile work. This 'Version 2.0 and 3.0' of her career added dots to connect later.

But after a few years, Adeline found herself craving more purpose and impact again. An insightful question from a coach crystalized her thinking:

'What would your eighty-year-old self thank you for doing today?'

Adeline's immediate answer? 'Not climbing the corporate ladder for more titles or money. But contributing value to others.'

It was time for a change.

Turning a Dream into a Reality

Adeline decided to take another career break, this time to write a book about the future of work—a topic she felt passionate about. She hoped the book would help brand herself for a return to corporate work.

But an unexpected thing happened.

The process of articulating her ideas and insights gave shape to a potential new career path—as a coach, helping professionals navigate the future economy.

Encouraged by positive feedback, Adeline decided to continue down the trail as a solopreneur instead of returning to corporate life.

It was uncharted territory. Her initial optimism soon met the messy reality of running a business. Without structure, Adeline found herself overwhelmed and racing in different directions.

She realized the corporate skills so ingrained in her could provide the missing scaffolding. Approaching her new venture like a start-up, Adeline set KPIs and created a business plan—her usual toolkit as a marketer.

But strangely, going through these corporate motions felt draining. In a moment of clarity, Adeline saw that progress couldn't be reduced to dollars and dashboards.

Impact was the metric that really mattered

When she reframed success as transforming lives, rather than hitting revenue goals, Adeline found her motivation again.

Learning to Flourish Out of the Corporate Greenhouse

Despite second-guessing herself along the way, Adeline has grown her career coaching services steadily over the past year.

But being a solopreneur requires new disciplines she didn't need in corporate life.

Adeline had to learn to work 'on' her business, not just 'in' it. Doing activities that don't immediately generate revenue but build long-term value—like developing her personal brand.

She also created structure to avoid burnout, timeboxing her days and keeping weekends work-free.

At the same time, Adeline leveraged her existing skills in marketing—now applied to promoting her own services. Activities like writing articles, public speaking, and networking allowed her to organically build credibility and visibility.

Ultimately mindset mattered most. Adeline adopted an attitude of curiosity rather than certainty. She gave herself permission to try new things, stumble, and course correct.

The Independence Payoff

Despite the challenges, Adeline has found deep fulfilment in self-employment that her corporate roles couldn't provide.

She relishes the freedom to choose who she works with and which projects to take on. Her time feels directed purely towards what energizes her.

While Adeline's income is now more variable, she's realized her actual cost of living is lower than imagined. And there is demand for her services, giving financial confidence.

Beyond the flexibility and freedom, being a solopreneur allows Adeline to align career and purpose like never before. Her work is now the impact she wished for.

Key Takeaways

- **Embrace incremental change:** Don't wait for a giant leap—incremental steps like career breaks and exploring passions can pave the way to self-employment.
- **Find your purpose:** Define success beyond money and titles. Aligning your work with impact and helping others can be a powerful motivator.
- **Leverage existing skills:** Your corporate expertise can be repurposed for building and running your solopreneur business.
- **Embrace the unstructured:** Adapt to the flexibility of self-employment by setting your own boundaries, prioritizing long-term value and learning to manage without rigid structures.
- **Find fulfilment in freedom:** Choose projects and clients that inspire you, control your time, and enjoy the satisfaction of aligning your career with your personal values.

Chapter 10

Mastering Productivity

'You cannot work 40 hours for other people, so you decided to work 100 hours for yourself.'

—Wife of a fellow entrepreneur

In his insightful article for the *Pensacola News Journal* titled 'Show me your calendar, and I'll tell you your priorities,' business leader Quint Studer dives into the fascinating link between our time management and our true priorities (Studer, 2018). He argues that examining our calendars reveals where we truly invest our energy and focus, often exposing hidden discrepancies between our stated goals and our daily actions. This thought-provoking piece challenges us to consciously design our schedules to reflect our aspirations and values, rather than letting them passively dictate our days.

It all started with an article in *Harvard Business Review* titled 'The Leader's Calendar: How CEOs Manage Time' (Nohria, 2018). Written by renowned strategist Michael E. Porter and his colleague Nitin Nohria, it documented a compelling twelve-year study analysing how twenty-seven CEOs navigate their work and personal time.

While the study confirmed that most CEOs possess clear and effective agendas, it also revealed a surprising statistic: on average, these CEOs attended thirty-seven meetings per week, consuming a staggering 72 per cent of their total work time. That's a lot of meetings—and potentially, a lot of time not spent where it mattered most.

And where did it matter most? Spending time with their customers—a mere 3 per cent of their time. This stark contrast highlights a potential disconnect between CEO priorities and the true drivers of business success.

It's easy to fall into the trap of 'frivolous time sucks', especially when you forge your own path and lack a clear-cut manual for success. I'm not suggesting that adhering to these findings guarantees instant achievement—as Psychology Professor Barry Schwartz reminds us in his TED talk, luck plays a significant role in our journeys (Schwartz, 2020).

But that doesn't mean we should abandon ourselves to chance. Just like seasoned athletes, we can inch towards success by focusing on the fundamentals: careful planning, deliberate training, and preparation for unexpected scenarios. By mastering these basic elements, we build a solid foundation to capitalize on both opportunity and luck when they arrive.

This is the thesis of Bill Walsh, one of the greatest coaches in NFL history and it is best epitomized in the title of his book—*The Score Takes Care of Itself* (Bill Walsh, 2010).

In the self-employment arena, it is best to optimize your working hours. One of the best approaches for me is timeboxing.

A concept best popularized by Nir Eyal, a bestselling author and behavioural scientist known for his work on habit formation, timeboxing is a time management technique that involves planning your day in advance by assigning specific time slots for each task or activity (Eyal, 2019). By timeboxing your schedule, you can reduce distractions, prioritize your most important work, align your actions with your values, and measure your progress.

Timeboxing is a simple but effective technique that can help you manage your time better and achieve your goals. Here are the basic steps to follow:

- Step 1: Identify your values and life domains. These are the areas of your life that are important to you, such as work, health, family, hobbies. PositivePsychology.com has a Setting Valued Goals[1] worksheet to help you reflect what you deem truly important in life so you can then set goals based on them.
- Step 2: Plan your week in advance. Use a calendar app or a paper planner to assign specific time slots for each of your tasks and activities. Make sure to include time for your values and life domains, as well as for rest and leisure. You can use a tool like Schedule Maker to help you create a timeboxed calendar (Eyal, Schedule Maker: Use this Google Sheet to Plan Your Week, n.d.).
- Step 3: Follow your plan and review your progress. Try to stick to your timeboxed schedule as much as possible, but be flexible and adaptable if things change. At the end of each day and week, review how well you followed your plan and what you accomplished. You can use a tool like RescueTime[2] to help you track and analyse your time usage.

By timeboxing your schedule, you can take control of your attention and choose how you spend your time. You can also reduce distractions, prioritize your most important work, align your actions with your values, and measure your progress. A tool like Clockify[3] can not only help you with timeboxing but to time track where you are spending your time.

---

[1] https://positive.b-cdn.net/wp-content/uploads/Setting-Valued-Goals.pdf

[2] https://www.rescuetime.com/

[3] https://clockify.me/timeboxing

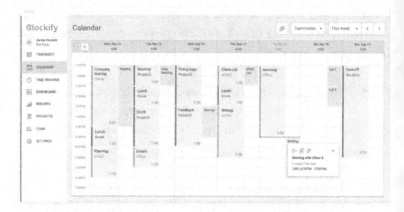

I would suggest doing it progressively instead of going for a tightly fitted Tetris as I first tried when I dove too deep into timeboxing.

Because you will lead to another problem and that is not catering for life's exigencies. You don't want to miss the first block and having everything snowball and affect everything else downstream. For me, it added unnecessary stress as I kept playing catch up and that meant sacrificing my lunch and break time.

In a recent viral post, solopreneur Justin Welsh outlined his 'perfect day', a meticulously planned routine featuring early wake-ups, intense workouts, and focused productivity (Welsh, n.d.).

But he also ended by saying that it is all a made-up fairy tale. That we won't possibly be able to achieve our perfect day, every single time. And it's okay. As he puts it, 'Life is a marathon, not a string of 10,000 perfect days put together.'

Working Smarter, Not Just Harder

For self-employed solopreneur like me, you only have twenty-four hours a day and truly nothing more. In a corporate world, you can have more than twenty-four hours because you can delegate and tap into other peoples' hours.

This is where the treasure trove of productivity tools come into the picture and help you scale your work, reduce your admin, and shave more margin off your life so you can focus on the important stuff that cannot be automated.

I started this journey just after I started CareerLadder. As a former business owner turned first-time solopreneur, it was overwhelming initially. I was accustomed to dishing out instructions and having others do the legwork for me.

Now I have to do my own legwork and I barely have time for other more important aspects of the business as I was mired in administrative quicksand.

Some of the common administrative quicksand includes:

- Setting up appointments with prospects, clients, and suppliers. There is usually the email ping-pong that goes on before a date and time that works for all parties can finally be identified.
- Sending chasers. Your clients are busy people and they may drop the ball. That means you need to nudge them to ensure they keep you top of mind and possibly influence the expedition of necessary actions from them. If you have many clients (a good problem), you may overlook the timely reminders you need to send them. Or worse, forget about them entirely.
- Keeping on top of tasks. As new things pile in, you need to make sure you are on top of things and nothing falls through the crack. There is only so much space for your Post-it notes before you run out of space. Or a gust of strong winds blows some with critical information under your table, compounding into a painful opportunity costs.
- Repetitive emails (see Sending Chasers) that are mostly the same with just a change to the salutation. If you have to do at scale, there is a lot of copying and pasting. It

is almost guaranteed that some of the first name would
not be adjusted properly. And worse, you found out only
after you send out that email!

These are some of the things you can expect to handle when you
are in self-employment mode. You can choose to outsource them
if you have the budget (more on that) but the first plan should
be to automate/scale them as much as possible with the existing
suite of technology.

Avoiding Productivity Pitfalls

As a solopreneur, efficiency is key to your success. Without proper
systems and processes, tasks pile up and productivity plummets.
Follow these fundamental strategies to avoid common pitfalls
and maximize your effectiveness.

Lacking or Ignoring a Business Plan

'Failing to plan is planning to fail.' This holds especially true
for solopreneurs who lack the support structures of a larger
organization.
      A solid business plan will:

- Outline your vision and goals to guide decision-making
  and resource allocation. Keeping your long-term objectives
  top of mind will increase productivity and focus.
- Define your target market, ensuring all efforts centre
  around serving the customers most likely to buy from
  you. Avoid wasting time on ineffective marketing or
  product development.
- List the milestones and key metrics you'll use to
  measure progress. This provides needed structure and
  accountability for a solopreneur prone to task-switching.

The simple act of writing a plan down helps crystallize your thinking and prime your mind for productivity. Periodically review your plan to check if you're on track and make adjustments as needed.

Begin with the end in mind, as author Stephen R. Covey cited in *The 7 Habits of Highly Effective People* (Covey, 2020). Imagine your ideal three-to-five-year outcome, then work backwards to the initial steps. This helps you focus resources on the highest priorities from the start.

Get a notebook and block out thirty to sixty minutes to draft:

• Your vision and goals for the next one to three years
• Your target customer personas
• The milestones and metrics that matter.

Having any map, even a rough sketch, is exponentially better than wandering map-less as so many solopreneurs do.

The 80/20 rule

Also known as the Pareto principle, it is a phenomenon that states that roughly 80 per cent of outcomes come from 20 per cent of causes. In other words, a small percentage of causes have an outsized effect. This concept is important to understand because it can help you identify which initiatives to prioritize so you can make the most impact.

Back in 1896, an Italian economist named Vilfredo Pareto noticed something curious. While studying land ownership in Italy, he discovered a startling imbalance: a mere 20 per cent of the population controlled a whopping 80 per cent of the land. This wasn't an isolated observation. Peering into his own garden, he found a similar pattern unfolding—a select 20 per cent of his plants were yielding a staggering 80 per cent of the fruit.

This lopsided relationship, where a small input disproportionately impacts the output, fascinated Pareto. He formalized it as the '80/20 rule' or the Pareto principle, a mathematical concept known as a power law distribution. Think of it as a tango between two quantities, where one partner's dramatic moves trigger significant shifts in the other.

You can use the 80/20 rule to prioritize the tasks that you need to get done during the day.

The idea is that out of your entire task list, completing 20 per cent of those tasks will result in 80 per cent of the impact you can create for that day. To maximize impact, choose the tasks with the biggest pay-off for your team and prioritize them for the day. Do any of your tasks involve collaborating with other teammates? Are there any tasks on your plate that are blocking projects from moving forward? These tasks may be simple in execution, but they can make a large impact to the rest of the team by allowing the process to keep flowing.

Avoid Shiny New Objects

Shiny object syndrome is the phenomenon of being distracted by new and exciting opportunities. For entrepreneurs, this can mean new business ideas, or products or services that aren't part of their current business plan. They have an urge to try this new thing that someone seems to be doing successfully. Realizing you are experiencing shiny object syndrome means admitting that your focus is waning and you're being pulled away by possibility and a fear of missing out.

We have probably seen a fair share of people pursuing shiny new objects at the height of the blockchain fever where companies did Initial Coins Offerings and NFT. Some of those companies have since moved into the current AI phase.

Imagine a straight path from where you are to your destination. It would be an easy commute from point A to point B and it probably would take you minutes. But every few steps along the way, you speak with the neighbours, you pick a few flowers, you kick around a bit with the kids. By the time you realize it, you are not even halfway there.

Imagine Superman being asked to help with your garden instead of battling Lex Luthor. Sounds absurd, right? Yet, many of us get caught in similar situations, saying 'yes' to every opportunity that comes our way, even if it diverts us from our true strengths and goals.

It's tempting to follow advice like Dr Atul Gawande's TED Talk suggestion: 'Say yes until you're 40, then say no.' His logic resonates—in our younger years, exploration is key. Saying 'yes' allows us to discover what energizes us and what doesn't. But this approach requires a crucial caveat: saying no when it matters most.

I learned this lesson the hard way. Early in my career, financial concerns drove me to say yes to everything. Two teaching gigs, a fractional CMO role, two content retainers, my podcasting . . . juggling all that became a logistical nightmare. Quality suffered, one project fell through, and I neglected the teaching job. In hindsight, saying no to that early on would have allowed me to prioritize projects I truly valued and deliver better results across the board.

The key takeaway isn't a blanket 'no' after forty. It's about strategic prioritizing: learning to distinguish the Lex Luthors from the gardening requests. Saying yes to opportunities that align with your strengths and goals, and confidently saying no to anything that would drain your time and energy—regardless of your age.

Remember, just like Superman wouldn't neglect Metropolis to weed your lawn, prioritizing what matters most allows you to be your best self in all aspects of your life.

My Productivity Tool Stack

These are software applications or online services that help people perform their tasks more efficiently and effectively.

They can be used for various purposes, such as planning, organizing, communicating, collaborating, creating, and managing projects.

Productivity tools are popular because they can provide many benefits to individuals and teams, such as:

- Saving time and reducing errors by automating or simplifying common tasks.
- Improving focus and concentration by limiting distractions and notifications.
- Enhancing creativity and innovation by providing templates, suggestions, and feedback.
- Increasing collaboration and communication by allowing easy sharing and editing of information.
- Boosting motivation and satisfaction by setting goals, tracking progress, and rewarding achievements.

Productivity tools can help people achieve their personal and professional goals more easily and enjoyably. They can also improve the quality and quantity of their work outcomes.

After years of experimenting and testing out more than hundreds of productivity tools, I more or less found the stack that works well for me. As someone who does not know how to code, I gravitate towards things that are really easy to pick up and feel intuitive from day one.

If you like to keep tab on all the newest and latest productivity tools, I suggest subscribing to the daily newsletter from Product Hunt[4]. It sends out a curated list of the top tools that are trending for the day.

I will check out the ones that resonate with me and play around to see what I think. It can be another rabbit hole if you are

---

[4] https://www.producthunt.com/

not careful. If you prefer to just start with what I have adopted, you can begin with the following stack.

And most of them are free or free-ish (they come with paid upgrades).

Before we begin, there are pre-requisites necessary for some of these tools to make sense:

1. A proper email account: By proper, I mean it is one powered by Google or Microsoft. You can get those cheap ones that come with your web hosting provider or even a free one from Zoho[5]. But if you wish to use a free calendaring tool, you need to have a better one (either Google or Microsoft).

2. A domain: Even if you are not picking up many assignments like I do, it is good to have an online presence to keep up with brand awareness and potentially inbound leads. A domain is just part of it as it means you have a unique URL that belongs to you. Personally I have adriantan. com.sg, which is my blog, and my business URL is marketingsumo.co. Depending on the domain level you are aiming for (.com, .com.sg, .sg), you should be able to secure most of them from GoDaddy[6] or Namecheap[7].

3. A website: Likely the domain vendor can also provide you with website support. GoDaddy does that and you can easily create a WordPress[8] site in a few clicks.

With those sorted out, you are ready to begin your tech stack adoption. Here are what I would call the starter kit that likely will make sense for you regardless of the nature of your business.

---

[5] https://www.zoho.com/mail/

[6] https://www.godaddy.com/

[7] https://www.namecheap.com/

[8] https://wordpress.com/

1. zcal:[9] This website connects with your google or Microsoft calendar and provides you with a dedicated calendar page that you can share with your contacts. To make an appointment with you, they just need to pick from the available slots and hit submit. On the backend, you can define when you are free or not. It will also track your existing calendars so if you are already busy for the entire Tuesday, that day will not be made available. No double booking.

2. followupthen.com:[10] If you know how to use email, you would know how to use followupthen. As the name implies, it help you with follow ups. Something that will be a constant occurrence in your business endeavour. Say you wish to send your contact an email follow-up on 1 October. If you are already sending an email, simply include 1oct@followupthen.com in the cc. An automated email will trigger when it hits the actual day. Or if you prefer to just notify yourself, simply move the same email address to bcc instead. You can even use other naming conventions such as 3days@followupthen.com (trigger in 3 days time) or a specific day such as monday@followupthen.com. No more manual to-do entries or reminders since you baked that into your email.

3. Magical:[11] Since clients and leads will typically go through the same sales cycle, the messaging to them will be vastly similar. Depending on your playbook, it may be an email or LinkedIn message to arrange for consultation call/Zoom, sharing of decks and pricing, and (likely) lots of chasers to expedite deal closure. I used to have these canned message templates in a Google Doc and

---

[9] zcal.co

[10] followupthen.com

[11] Getmagical.com

copy/paste over. Multiply that by the number of emails and that is easily fifteen to twenty minutes of your day.

4. Bing AI:[12] This is Microsoft Bing's version of ChatGPT, which also has a better interface, but less features, than ChatGPT. It is powered by GPT4, the latest Large Language Model, which basically means it uses the internet as its source of knowledge and can generate natural and engaging conversations with users like yourself. I use the Creative mode and it helps me with the first draft of everything from a blog title to social media caption to even long-form blog post. The best part is you can make it write in your own style. Just feed it with content you wrote before and have it decipher and describe your writing style. In future outputs—and you must do this every time because Bing AI is forgetful—remember to include the writing style at the end of your new requests.

5. Grammarly:[13] English isn't my native language even though it is my first. When you got to be quick with correspondence, you don't want to spend too much time being a grammar Nazi over your message. Grammarly is like an advanced version of spellcheck but it also advice tonality as well as style if one is indicated in the app.

6. ChatGPT Summary for Chrome:[14] This is for the Chrome users. Constant learning is a way to improve your craft as a self-employed. This may mean reading up on articles, watching free YouTube videos to pick up new skills. But being self-employed also means you are time tight. Before you may want to deep dive and spend

---

[12] Bing.com

[13] Grammarly.com

[14] chromewebstore.google.com/detail/chatgpt-summary-for-chrom/mikcekmbahpbehdpakenaknkkedeonhf

twenty minutes reading a long-form article or watch a video, you can use this Chrome app to create summary so you can get the gist of things before you commit more time to it.

7. Microsoft To Do:[15] Most to-do list apps operate quite simply and function more or less the same. This is just one of those that I stopped toying around with since the possible gain from another new app is marginal. I've been using this app from the time when it Wunderlist, before Microsoft bought it a few years ago. Since then, the app is infused with other Microsoft products but my main use is still as a To-Do list. You can have different categories—I have work, tasks, and even shopping list—and you can even share the list with others (I share my shopping list with my family). It also allows you to set reminders and star tasks so as to prioritize them accordingly.

There are many more that I use but their use cases are not related to either marketing or sales. I will share more about them in the respective marketing and sales chapters.

And while these apps work for me, they may be more of a hindrance to you. It depends on your own preference and workflows. One thing is for sure, they definitely help you to become more efficient. Whether it comes in the form of my recommendation or something else, it is important to make use of technology as much as possible so you can save more time for more important stuffs.

Key Takeaways

- Productivity techniques alone are not enough—it's important to also set boundaries and schedule non-work

---

[15] to-do.office.com/tasks/

time to recharge and avoid burnout. Parkinson's Law teaches us that work expands to fill the available time, so leaving room for rest is crucial.

- Timeboxing your schedule can help prioritize important tasks and values while reducing distractions. It works best when done progressively rather than too rigidly to allow flexibility for life's unexpected events.

- Automation tools like zcal, FollowUpThen, and Magical can save significant time on repetitive administrative and sales/marketing tasks by streamlining workflows.

- Proper planning with goals and metrics in a business plan provides needed structure for solopreneurs who lack organizational support. It helps staying focused on what matters most.

- Prioritizing tasks with the highest impact according to the 80/20 rule maximizes productivity. Saying no to unaligned opportunities is also important for maintaining focus on what really drives results.

Chapter 11

Achieving Work-Life Harmony

'Don't confuse having a career with having a life.'
—Hillary Clinton

In 2013, the then CEO of LinkedIn, Jeff Weiner, wrote a post on LinkedIn about the importance of scheduling nothing. Every week, his calendar has blocks of grey that he deliberately blocks out. Nothing is happening during those blocks. It is blocked out so he can do his thinking and reflection.

To him, scheduling 'buffers' or time slots with no meetings is a crucial productivity tool that allows one to think strategically, recharge, and regain control of their day. Jeff allocates ninety minutes to two hours daily for buffers, allowing time for coaching and strategic thinking.

This is because strategic thinking requires uninterrupted focus and time for developing ideas and scenarios. The buffer time is an investment in oneself and a crucial productivity tool.

It is somewhat like the annual corporate retreat but done in weekly bite-sized slots. Being self-employed can make you become really busy overnight. It may mean so deep on the factory floor that you have no idea that the customers have left the building.

Having time to think, to reflect, and to ponder what could be done better and what are the projects that need adjustment is a superpower that anyone of us can tap into as long as we have the gumption to make sure it happens.

For me, I have my weekly session every Sunday afternoon when I'm most chill. I would:

1. Review the week just past
2. Review the next two weeks ahead
3. Revisit my goals
4. Revisit my to-do list
5. Choose my top three outcomes for the week ahead
6. Schedule the time to work against those outcomes as appointments in my calendar

The last bit is the most important for me. Without corporate guardrails, it is easy to fall into distractions around you. I have programmed myself to more or less defer to my preset calendar on what I need to do for that day.

If adherence is a struggle, try to gamify it and have a reward after each accomplishment. As an avid drinker, I've created a unique reward system to motivate myself: I only allow myself to indulge if I've had a workout that day. It's a win-win situation! The exercise keeps me healthy and focused, and the anticipation of that post-workout drink adds a delicious layer of motivation. Plus, in Singapore's scorching heat and humidity, the air-conditioned gym becomes even more tempting!

Failing to Establish Efficient Processes and Workflows

Entrepreneur Michael Gerber shared the story of a client who owned three dry cleaners (Gerber, 2004). Despite working sixty to seventy hours a week, he felt perpetually overwhelmed as he did everything himself with no systems.

Once he implemented processes to define tasks, train employees, and automate routines, productivity soared and work-life balance improved dramatically.

Take the time upfront to lay out your rough goals, strategies, and milestones—it will save you from floundering later. As author Srinivas Rao says, 'The discipline of writing things down, of converting your thoughts and goals into a clear and concise plan of action, makes them more real and gives you energy.' (Rao, 2017)

So grab a pen and paper, or open a document on your laptop. Outline your vision for how you want your business to grow, the customers you want to serve, and the impact you want to make. Even the process of writing it down will prime your brain for productivity. Then revisit your plan regularly to check your progress and course correct as needed. A solid plan will keep you focused and efficient, so you can make the most of your time as a solopreneur.

You can build efficient systems by:

- Creating templates and checklists
- Implementing project management software
- Automating routine communication
- Outsourcing non-essential tasks
- Hiring part-time or temporary help

Together, these systems maximize your productivity and minimize wasted time, freeing you up for more meaningful work and life. Focus on high-leverage tasks that only you can accomplish.

Underestimating Time Required for Non-Revenue Activities

You likely underestimate how long administrative tasks take as a solopreneur. Handling finances, customer support, ordering supplies, and more consume significant portions of your week that add up quickly.

Entrepreneur Tai Lopez recommends classifying your work into three categories:

- $10 Work: Tasks anyone can do like email, social media, and basic admin.
- $100 Work: Non-creative work that requires some skill like customer support, drafting contracts, and payroll.
- $1000 Work: Your unique expertise and creative output that grows the business-like content creation, product development, and high-level strategy.

Here are some ways to identify which tasks are $10, $100, and $1,000 work as a solopreneur:

$10 work:

- Requires little to no expertise or specialized skill
- Can be done quickly and easily by almost anyone
- Is repetitive and does not provide much variety

Examples: Social media posting, data entry, responding to basic customer emails, filing paperwork

$100 work:

- Requires some competency, knowledge, or specialized training
- Deals with operational tasks that support the business
- Does not leverage your unique expertise or creative abilities

Examples: Handling customer service escalations, scheduling appointments, processing payments, drafting standard legal documents

$1,000 work:

- Leverages your unique skills, experiences, and creative abilities
- Involves strategic thinking, problem-solving, and decision-making
- Has a direct impact on growing the business and serving customers in a high-value way

Examples: Creating high-value content, developing new products/services, pitching to potential partners, advising clients, recruiting talent.

To identify the type of work you do:

- Audit how you currently spend your time
- Ask yourself for each task: 'Could someone else do this relatively easily?'
- Categorize tasks based on the expertise/skill required, complexity, strategic importance, and impact on growth.

Then prioritize automating/outsourcing $10 work, hiring help for $100 work, and protecting ample time for $1,000 work that only you can do to further your business. Focus on tasks that leverage your unique strengths as a solopreneur.

Tim Ferriss shares the story of an entrepreneur who thought emails would take only two to three hours per week (Ferriss, 2016). In reality, it consumed ten to fifteen hours. You must identify where your actual minutes go, then adjust.

Success lies in properly budgeting time for 'support' tasks in your schedule while prioritizing $1,000 work:

- Automate repeatable $10 tasks using software and templates.

- Outsource $10 tasks that do not require your unique skills.
- Block out chunks of focused time for $1,000 work like planning, content creation, and product development.
- Hire virtual or part-time assistants to handle $100 work that eats up your time.

With realistic schedules and efficient systems in place, you'll avoid being consumed by $10 and $100 tasks at the expense of higher value $1,000 work. Time management and streamlined processes enable you to make the biggest impact and get the most from your solopreneur journey.

Achieving Work-Life Nirvana

Many assume self-employed people must 'always hustle' with no end in sight. This myth leads solopreneurs to burn out—missing the benefits of proper rest, boundaries, and downtime.

It does not help that I work from home so I work where I live. The line between work and life is non-existent. That is why so many people suffered from burnout during the peak of COVID-19 when most of us were forced to work from home.

We would think it is just one more email or one more WhatsApp, but it often does not stop there. Because since you already have your devices, you might as well check your inbox, refresh your LinkedIn feed, or double-check your to-do list.

It was down this spiral that led me to the occasional burnout. Luckily for me, I have clear symptoms when I'm on that path. I tend to get fidgety as if I overdose on caffeine. That is my alarm bell to dial it back down.

And really, do we want to work 100 hours for ourselves? Perhaps it could be what you wish to optimize for and good for you. But one of the many things I enjoy from self-employment is the freedom to spend my weekdays not working.

This was seeded in me when I was working in a call centre where we had to work in shifts and we got rest days on weekdays instead. Spending leisure time on weekdays avoided the typical weekend crowd and peak period, making downtime so much more enjoyable.

So if you are like me, forget the myths and discover how to achieve your work-life nirvana.

Set Work Boundaries to Recharge

Sri Sri Ravi Shankar emphasizes the importance of rest in fuelling creativity: 'The moments of stillness in our mind are the moments of creativity and innovation (Shankar, 2021). To come up with your best ideas, you must recharge.

Yet during self-employment, switching 'off' can feel impossible. Unanswered emails, unfiled receipts, and unfinished projects loom. But unstructured time allows space for new insights to emerge.

So set work boundaries that signal 'done for the day'. Use an out-of-office message when logging off, turn alerts off on devices, and delegate anything that cannot wait. Create a ritual to signify transitioning from work to personal time.

There are a few ways this can be done. My current practice is to have a Shutdown calendar event that triggers every weekday at 4.30 p.m. That is my signal to start winding down, review my calendar for the next day, and also to clock in on any top priorities I should start my next day with.

If it works better for you, you can set it as a recurring alarm on your watch or phone for the same effect.

Sometimes work boundaries can be harder to manage if it involves your clients. Perhaps they have a habit of contacting you after office hours. Or maybe they want to meet when it is time to send your kids to school. It is a hard beam to balance.

Setting initial expectations is helpful. This means letting your clients know during onboarding about your business hours. It will set expectations about when you are and are not available.

If your nature of business requires you to be on social media a lot, use an automated away message on social media when you're taking a break, directing clients to your website for inquiries.

And don't feel you have to respond immediately to texts and messages. Responding only during your business hours helps set the expectation that you're not available at all times.

Lastly, some of those 'urgent' questions might appear to be a recurring theme across leads and customers. It will take a bit more effort to front load it but having FAQs on your website will minimize and reduce the amount of time you spend repeating the same thing in person.

These boundaries allow your mind and body to restore, prepping you for better work tomorrow. The muse visits those who make room for her. Innovation demands the breaks in between.

Practise 'Scheduled Ignorance'

'Scheduled ignorance' is a term coined by Shane Parrish, the founder of Farnam Street, a website that helps people master the best of what other people have already figured out (Ferriss, 2023). It refers to the deliberate choice of avoiding certain information or sources of distraction that are not relevant, useful, or meaningful for your goals or well-being.

According to Parrish, scheduled ignorance can help you focus on what matters, reduce mental clutter, and avoid information overload.

Some examples of scheduled ignorance are:

- Turning off notifications on your phone or computer. Notifications can interrupt your flow and tempt you to check your messages, social media, or news feeds. By turning them off, you can reduce the amount of noise and distraction in your environment and choose when to engage with them.

- Unfollowing or muting people on social media who are negative, toxic, or uninteresting.
- Reading books or articles that are relevant to your interests or goals, rather than browsing random or sensationalized content.
- Limiting your exposure to news or media that are biased, inaccurate, or sensationalized.
- Scheduling time to worry or stress about things that are beyond your control, rather than letting them consume your attention throughout the day.
- Unsubscribe from newsletters, podcasts, or blogs that are not adding value to your life.
- Schedule time for learning and entertainment.
- Practise mindfulness and meditation.

Scheduled ignorance is not the same as wilful ignorance, which is the refusal to acknowledge or accept facts or evidence that contradict your beliefs or opinions. Wilful ignorance can lead to overconfidence, poor judgment, and irrational behaviour. Scheduled ignorance, on the other hand, is a conscious and strategic decision to filter out the noise and focus on the signal.

Becoming your own boss offers boundless freedom. But with great power comes great responsibility. You must be vigilant about self-care and intentional work-life integration to avoid burnout.

Create structure while retaining flexibility. Use time-blocking and calendar scheduling to protect priorities and deep-focus work. Schedule space rather than back-to-back meetings.

Establish work boundaries and end-of-day rituals that signal shutting off. Protect time for rest, relationships, and rejuvenation. Your productivity tomorrow depends on proper rest today.

Leverage tools and systems to eliminate inefficiencies. Delegate or outsource tasks misaligned with your genius zone. Embrace automation to free up mental bandwidth.

Continuous learning prevents stagnation. Allot time regularly for reading, online courses, and podcasts. Acquiring new skills and perspectives boosts creativity.

Remember the journey is a marathon, not sprint. With balance and self-care, you generate sustainable energy to keep chasing milestones.

Making intentional choices allows work and life to coexist in harmony. With diligence, you can build routines that energize rather than deplete you. Prioritize self-compassion.

You now have insights and techniques tailor a schedule that aligns work and purpose. Protecting your peace and energy liberates you to make the impact only you are capable of making.

Key Takeaways

- Set clear boundaries between work and personal time by establishing defined hours for when you are 'on' and 'off' work. Use rituals like shutting down your laptop or changing your status on messaging platforms to clearly signal the transition.
- Schedule protected time blocks daily/weekly to prioritize work that needs focus where you free yourself from distractions and avoid back-to-back meetings that leave no room for reflection or downtime.
- Employ techniques like 'scheduled ignorance' where you deliberately filter out and avoid needless distractions outside work hours, like turning off notifications on devices and muting unhelpful social circles.
- Automate routine tasks, outsource administrative work, and delegate responsibilities that don't require your

unique skills and expertise as much as possible to free up significant time.

- Balance work with adequate rest, meaningful personal relationships, continuous learning, and activities that boost your mental and physical well-being; prioritizing self-care ensures sustainability and harmony over both your work and personal life in the long-run.

Chapter 12

Structuring Your Business Entity and Legal Considerations

'The difference between something good and something great is attention to detail.'
—Charles R. Swindoll

When I first embarked on my self-employment journey, one of the first daunting tasks was determining how to legally structure my business. As a corporate veteran used to having employees handle regulatory frameworks, I suddenly felt adrift in uncharted legal seas.

Should I simply operate as a sole proprietorship using my NRIC? Or enter into a partnership with a co-founder to share ownership? Perhaps it made more sense to incorporate a private limited company for liability protection? My lack of expertise on these matters gave me plenty of restless nights in the beginning.

After discussions with fellow solopreneurs and researching options online, I concluded incorporating a private limited company in Singapore was the optimal approach. This required drafting a constitution and completing the necessary paperwork for ACRA and IRAS, which my corporate secretarial services provider Sleek handled smoothly.

While incorporating had higher upfront costs, I realized limiting my personal liability was crucial as a one-man business. Transferring legal risk to the company entity gave me invaluable peace of mind. Opening a corporate bank account also conveyed a professional image to clients.

Additionally, the corporate tax structure allowed some strategic tax planning by splitting my income across personal and business. While I barely understood tax issues at first, my accountants patiently explained how to minimize my obligations over the long run.

Despite some frustrating red tape dealing with government agencies initially, I'm grateful I made the effort upfront to properly structure and register my enterprise. The corporate veil has already shielded me during some unexpected business hiccups over the years.

Looking back, I am thankful I invested time researching the options and seeking advice early on. The right business structure provided a robust foundation to build upon. My naivety around legal and tax considerations could have landed me in hot water without the protective rails of incorporation.

Choosing a Business Structure

Selecting the right structure for your business is a foundational yet complex decision when embarking on self-employment. The options you choose from will vary based on your country and local regulations. Some common structures include:

Sole Proprietorship

The simplest option, where you as an individual directly own the business. No formal registration is required beyond licenses to operate. However, you assume unlimited personal liability for debts and legal claims associated with the business. All profits flow directly to you and are taxed as personal income.

Partnership

Two or more individuals jointly own and operate the business. General partnerships assume joint, unlimited liability while limited partnerships offer liability protection for 'silent' partners. Partners share profits according to predetermined ratios but also share personal liability. A formal partnership agreement is recommended to govern the relationships and responsibilities between partners.

Limited Liability Company (LLC)

One of the most popular corporate structures for small businesses in many countries. LLCs combine pass-through taxation benefits of a partnership with liability protections of a corporation. Profits pass through to members' personal tax returns. The personal assets of LLC members are shielded from business debts and liabilities.

Private Limited Company

A separately registered legal entity that fully separates the company from its shareholders. Owners' liability is limited to their investment in company shares. Considered lower risk than sole proprietorships or general partnerships since personal assets are fully protected. Perceived credibility with customers. Can raise funding through issuing shares. Disadvantage is higher legal and accounting compliance requirements.

Deciding on the appropriate structure involves weighing factors like liability protection needs, taxes, ownership flexibility, costs, and paperwork. Most common considerations include:

- Limiting your personal liability from the business
- Pass-through taxation benefits
- Separating personal and company assets/finances
- Projected profits and taxes

- Administrative requirements and compliance costs
- Future expansion plans
- Ownership structure (single vs multiple owners)

Accounting and Bookkeeping

Proper accounting and financial record-keeping are crucial for self-employed individuals. Unlike traditional employment, you become solely responsible for these operational aspects when working for yourself.

DIY vs Hiring Help

You can choose to handle your own basic bookkeeping using accounting software. This allows hands-on control and saves costs initially. However, consider hiring an accountant or bookkeeper if you dislike finance admin or as your business grows in complexity. Their expertise saves time and errors. Sleek also offers this as a value-added service.

Accounting Software

User-friendly accounting software automates tasks like tracking income and expenses, generating invoices, managing cash flow, and producing financial statements. Popular options include:

- QuickBooks – Robust features for small businesses. Integrates with many other business apps.
- Xero – Cloud-based with mobile apps. Best for service businesses.
- FreshBooks – Specialized for service professionals and freelancers. Very user-friendly.
- Wave – Free option. Best for very simple finances. Limited features.

Key Financial Records

Be diligent in recording all business transactions. Key documents to maintain include:

- Income and sales records (quotations, invoices, purchase orders, receipts, bank deposits)
- Expense records (purchases, bills, receipts, bank/credit card statements)
- Assets and liabilities (cash, loans, inventory, equipment, accounts receivable/payable,
- Payroll records and tax payments
- All other supporting documents (contracts, policies, inventory, etc.)

Cash vs Accrual Accounting

Understand the difference between cash basis and accrual accounting. Cash basis recognizes income/expenses when cash is received or paid. Accrual basis records them when transactions occur regardless of payment date. Accrual is more complex but gives a clearer financial picture.

Financial Statements

Regularly review key financial statements generated by your accounting system. This allows closely monitoring the financial health and performance of your business. Critical reports include:

- Income statement – Summary of revenue and expenses over a period. Shows profitability.
- Balance sheet – Snapshot of business assets, liabilities, and equity on a given date.
- Cash flow statement – Tracks money flowing in and out of your business from operations, investments, and financing.

Taxes

As a self-employed individual in Singapore, you need to be aware of your tax obligations to IRAS (Inland Revenue Authority of Singapore). This includes registering for GST (Goods and Services Tax), making income tax payments, and submitting annual tax returns.

Registering for GST

If your annual revenue exceeds S$1 million, you must register for GST. This requires submitting GST returns and payments to IRAS on a quarterly basis. GST registration allows you to claim GST paid on business expenses as input tax credit. Consider voluntary GST registration even if below the threshold to claim input tax.

Filing Estimated Chargeable Income

As a self-employed person in Singapore you must submit an Estimated Chargeable Income (ECI) declaration to IRAS within three months of your business financial year-end. Your ECI is used to calculate income tax payments for the next year. An instalment plan allows paying taxes due in fixed monthly amounts rather than a lump sum.

Making CPF Contributions

As a self-employed, you are responsible for both employer and employee CPF contributions. This totals up to 37 per cent of your monthly income. You must submit CPF contributions and declare your income to CPF Board. This ensures you remain covered by CPF pension, medical, home schemes.

Claiming Business Expense Deductions

You can deduct a wide range of business expenses incurred to generate income. Examples include office rental, utilities, accounting fees, staff salaries, advertising, software costs, transportation, and asset depreciation. However, you must maintain documentation to prove business use only.

Filing Annual Income Tax Returns

You must file an Annual Income Tax Return declaring all income received. This is submitted along with supporting documents for expenses claimed. IRAS will assess taxes owed based on your chargeable income after deductions.

Using a Tax Agent

Consider engaging a qualified tax agent to prepare your ECI, GST returns, and annual income tax filing. They can ensure compliance, maximize lawful deductions, and avoid errors that lead to penalties. Expect fees of a few hundred dollars.

Insurance Considerations

When self-employed, you lose access to employer-provided insurance benefits. This makes securing coverage on your own crucial to protect your business and personal assets. Common policies include:

General Liability Insurance

Covers costs if a third party sues your business for property damage or bodily injury caused by your operations, products, services, or employees.

Professional Liability Insurance

Also called errors and omissions (E&O) insurance. Protects against claims of losses/damages suffered by clients caused by negligence or failure to deliver services. Essential for consultants.

Cyber/Data Breach Insurance

Safeguards against expenses related to cyberattacks on your systems that compromise sensitive customer data. Provides funds for legal action, customer notifications, PR, and loss recovery.

Health Insurance

Options to obtain health insurance include purchasing a private plan, enrolling through a government insurance marketplace, or getting added to a spouse's employer policy.

Disability Insurance

Replaces income if injury or illness prevents you from working. Especially important given lack of employment benefits.

Life Insurance

Provide financial support for dependents in the event of untimely death. Term life insurance is an affordable option. Having life insurance helps secure business loans if required.

In addition, consider business property insurance if you have a home office or commercial location, commercial auto insurance for any company vehicles, and business interruption insurance to replace income lost due to events like natural disasters.

Check if your business lease or contracts obligate you to carry specific types or limits of coverage. An insurance broker can advise on optimal protection. Pay close attention to exclusions and limitations when reviewing policies.

Contracts and Legal Protection

Using contracts and formal agreements is crucial when taking on clients as a self-employed professional. Well-drafted contracts clarify expectations, duties, and intellectual property rights upfront to prevent misunderstandings down the road.

Key Contract Clauses

Your client contracts should cover terms like:

— Clearly defined scope of work and deliverables
— Timelines for completion of services
— Payment amounts, schedules, and invoicing logistics
— Handling changes in scope requests
— Ownership of intellectual property produced
— Confidentiality and non-disclosure
— Termination rights and consequences
— Liability limitations

Another way is to leverage samples and legal self-help resources when drafting your contracts.

Here are some recommended online resources for getting contract templates and sample agreements.

• DocPro:[1] Provides free customizable templates for contracts, proposals, invoices, NDAs, and more. Just select your industry and document type.
• Rocket Lawyer:[2] Offers a free seven-day trial to access their library of legal forms and contracts for small businesses. Has many different templates for services, sales, employment, and IP protection.
• LawDepot:[3] Has a free tier with access to essential templates. Paid plans unlock more customizable business contract templates.

---

[1] https://docpro.com/

[2] https://www.rocketlawyer.com/

[3] https://www.lawdepot.com/

- Contracts for Creatives:[4] Specialized site with free contract templates designed for self-employed creatives, artists, designers, etc. Includes sample consulting and copyright transfer agreements.
- Hello Bonsai:[5] Resources focused on freelance service providers. Download free, editable templates for statements of work, proposals, invoices, and more.

I'd recommend browsing a few of these sites to find templates closest to your needs that you can then customize further. Having good foundation documents makes tailoring your own contracts much easier.

Many of these may not be best suited to your country's specific legislation so as much as possible, do have a lawyer to review the draft.

The legal and organizational aspects of launching your venture may seem tedious compared to passion pursuits. But proper structuring provides the sturdy backbone for your dreams to thrive.

Invest time upfront choosing and forming the right business entity for your goals and risk profile. Limit personal liability through incorporation or other formal structures.

Use accounting software and bookkeeping systems to ensure financial integrity. Maintain meticulous records of income, expenses, assets, and obligations.

Learn your unique tax obligations as a self-employed individual. Work closely with professionals to maximize write-offs and avoid costly penalties or interest.

Protect your business interests through carefully drafted contracts, agreements, and insurance policies. Seek legal counsel when needed to safeguard your rights.

---

[4] https://ashleehightower.com/

[5] https://www.hellobonsai.com/

While not glamorous, addressing these operational necessities properly from the outset prevents major headaches later on. It allows focusing energy on service rather than distractions.

With robust legal and financial foundations in place, you are free to direct your passion and gifts towards higher aims. Your business flourishes when the infrastructure supports sustainable growth.

You now have guidance to strategically structure and fortify the legal underpinnings of your venture. Doing this diligent groundwork liberates you to ultimately soar unencumbered by administrative burdens.

Key Takeaways

- Determine your optimal business structure considering liability, taxation, ownership by choosing from sole proprietorships, partnerships, LLCs, or private limited companies. This provides a legal framework for your venture.

- Use bookkeeping software to automate income, expense tracking, and generate invoices while adhering to accounting standards. Outsource these tasks if complexity grows over time.

- File estimated income declarations and make compulsory CPF contributions on time to satisfy your tax obligations as a self-employed individual in Singapore.

- Deduct qualifying business expenses by maintaining documentation and working with tax agents to maximize deductions within the law.

- Secure essential business insurance like general liability, professional liability, cyber and health to mitigate risks while utilizing online resources and legal counsel to draft tailored contracts and agreements.

Part IV

Emotional Resilience and Motivation

From Retrenched to Reinvented: Steven Lock's Journey into Self-Employment

Losing your job is often seen as a catastrophe. But for Steven, getting retrenched from his corporate role at age forty-three ended up being a blessing in disguise (Lock, 2023). At first, the future looked bleak. Steven had devoted over twenty years to building a successful regional leadership career in IT. Identity and self-worth were intrinsically tied to his corporate status and achievements.

Like many who face retrenchment, Steven's initial reactions were fear and disbelief. How would he maintain his livelihood? Would he ever reclaim the stature he had attained?

But as the dust settled, Steven recognized he had come to a crossroad. He could try to get back on the corporate ladder in a similar role. Or he could use this unexpected change as a catalyst to pursue something entirely new.

Steven courageously chose the road less travelled. He stepped into the unknown, driven by a growing yearning for more meaning and impact in his work.

Trying On Different Hats as a Newly Minted Business Owner

In reinventing himself after retrenchment, Steven first tried to capitalize on his ample corporate experience. With over twenty years under his belt, he certainly had a vast repertoire of knowledge and skills to impart.

Training and consulting services seemed like an intuitive path for monetizing his expertise. But Steven soon realized that standing in front of rooms delivering content just didn't energize him. Neither did many other aspects of entrepreneurship come naturally. Networking felt awkward and disingenuous. Self-promotion didn't align with Steven's introverted tendencies, either.

Accustomed to having specialized support teams in corporate life, wearing all the hats of a business owner himself was uncomfortable. Steven was on a steep learning curve. Through trial and error, he pieced together a way forward. Steven tapped into social media, publishing regular long-form posts to establish thought leadership.

He pushed past his introversion to network in-person, forced out of his comfort zone to make the connections he needed. And to lead workshops, Steven even joined Toastmasters to hone public speaking abilities from scratch.

Slowly but surely, Steven built his personal brand and visibility, attracting a small client base. But it required relentlessly pushing past self-doubt and his limits.

Finding Flow and Meaning in an Unexpected New Career

The biggest revelation came when Steven discovered his love for coaching others. He uncovered that he had actually been doing informal coaching all along as a people leader.

Getting formally trained and certified in coaching felt aligned, like meeting a calling. Steven realized he had found a business model he could sustain for the long-term without burning out.

Coaching allowed Steven to leverage his experience and wisdom gained over decades in the corporate world. But the one-on-one, in-the-moment connection gave his work a renewed sense of purpose.

By focusing squarely on impacting others' lives in a meaningful way, Steven's work took on a whole new meaning. Financial metrics were replaced by human ones.

Today, Steven runs a thriving global coaching practice tailored exactly to his strengths. He has found harmony in work-life integration on his terms too.

Losing his job opened up new vistas Steven never could have imagined while climbing the corporate ladder. He is living proof that radical reinvention is possible.

Overcoming the Mental Roadblocks of Reinvention

Of course, Steven's journey into self-employment was far from easy. Becoming your own boss meant dismantling long-held assumptions.

As a corporate professional, Steven was wired to think in terms of career progression and titles. But business ownership is nonlinear and iterative.

The uncertainty of not having a clear path or established playbook was unsettling at first. Steven had to get comfortable with discovery rather than destination.

He also wished he better understood the financial realities of entrepreneurship earlier. Steven spent too much upfront establishing his first business. Learning to bootstrap came later. Most challenging was overcoming the mental roadblocks. Steven had to unmesh his personal identity from corporate status and shed the associated ego.

He found purpose in self-improvement rather than achievement, joy in the process rather than end goals. With this refreshed mindset, the other pieces fell into place.

Key Takeaways

- Losing his long-term corporate job was initially difficult for Steven, but ended up catalysing bold reinvention into a more meaningful new career path than he imagined possible.
- Steven had to try different business models leveraging his expertise before discovering his true calling in coaching, which allowed holistic client impact utilizing his experience.
- Pivoting to entrepreneurship required developing new skills like networking, self-promotion, and public speaking that didn't come naturally to Steven.
- Overcoming mental barriers like an identity tied to corporate status and assumptions about career progression was a challenge Steven had to address through mindset shifts.

By focusing on continual growth, living purposefully and finding joy in the journey rather than just goals, Steven was able to establish a fulfilling new path aligned with his strengths and values on his own terms.

Who you become after a major shake-up is entirely up to you. With courage, persistence, and a learner's mindset, you can create a whole new path aligned with your true calling. Steven's reinvention proves it's never too late to transform yourself.

Chapter 13

Coping with the Emotional Rollercoaster

'Courage doesn't always roar. Sometimes courage is the quiet voice at the end of the day saying "I will try again tomorrow".'
—Mary Anne Radmacher

Being an entrepreneur can be fun and exciting, but also scary and lonely. When I quit my corporate job to start my own business, I didn't know how hard it would be. I lost my confidence without any support or feedback from bosses or colleagues.

I felt like I was lost in the middle of nowhere, without the security of a regular income or a clear plan. I was stressed out by the bills that kept coming, more than what I was making from my new business. To avoid going broke, I took on more work, but it was too much to handle.

I felt worse when I saw how well other people were doing on social media. I wondered if I was good enough to succeed. I didn't see any hope or help ahead.

After months of not sleeping well and being distracted, I realized I had to change something. I started to meditate every day to calm down and focus. I said positive things to myself instead of negative ones when I looked in the mirror.

I reached out to other entrepreneurs and found out they were also struggling in different ways. I learned from their stories and how they overcame their challenges. I saw the light at the end of the tunnel that was my goal.

I still have a lot of work to do to get to where I want to be. But now I move forward with confidence, no matter what. Nothing can stop me, only make me stronger.

My journey as an entrepreneur reminds me of when I used to struggle to learn how to cycle as a kid. With hard work and courage, one can make the seemingly impossible possible.

Understanding the Self-Employment Mindset

Accepting Uncertainty

Becoming comfortable with uncertainty and nonlinear progress is critical as an entrepreneur, yet easier said than done. There is no predefined roadmap or the comfort of a regular pay cheque in self-employment. The path forward is often murky, requiring you to become agile and adaptable as circumstances change.

Uncertainty manifests in many forms—not knowing if your idea will find a market, unpredictable customer demand, sudden shifts in the competitive landscape, technology disruption, economic fluctuations. There are always factors outside your control.

Self-employment requires taking leaps of faith and having the resilience to course correct as challenges arise. The uncertainty can seem daunting at times.

It's important to celebrate small wins and milestones, not just the end goal. The journey is not linear—you will likely take two steps forward and one step back many times. But each small step brings you closer to your vision being realized.

When self-doubt creeps in, remember why you started this journey in the first place. Your passion and ingenuity can help you navigate uncertainty. Trust in your vision and abilities, while remaining flexible in your approach.

Everytime I get overwhelmed by new uncertainty, I bring myself back to the emotional moment when I decided to quit my last job and all the push factors behind it.

Facing the unknown requires mental strength and courage. But embracing uncertainty also makes the path personally rewarding, allowing you to evolve through the twists and turns. With dedication and agility, you can assemble your airplane even in free fall.

Risk Tolerance and Growth Mindset

Launching any new venture involves substantial risk. From financial uncertainty to competitive threats, challenges and setbacks are inevitable in entrepreneurship. You must develop resilience and a high tolerance for risk-taking to survive the twists and turns.

Making the leap into self-employment often requires giving up a stable income source. Recovering from business mistakes or failed product launches can be costly. There is no safety net.

Yet being too risk-averse can also doom your chances of success. As Mark Zuckerberg said, 'The biggest risk is not taking any risk' (Nucleus_AI, 2023). Carefully calculated risks and bold strategic bets are often needed to break through.

Having a growth mindset is essential, where skills and abilities can be developed over time through dedication and perseverance. View setbacks as learning experiences rather than failures. Ask yourself, 'What lessons can I take from this to improve?'

You may need to make dramatic pivots, but stay persistent in pursuit of your overall vision. Thomas Edison famously attempted thousands of filament designs before successfully inventing the incandescent light bulb (Roy, 2022). Had he given up prematurely, he would not have illuminated the world.

As an entrepreneur, you will be defined not by the challenges you face, but by how you respond to them. Maintain self-belief throughout the journey, letting passion and resilience drive you. The only true failure is allowing hardship to extinguish your entrepreneurial spirit before realizing your full potential.

Challenges and setbacks are inevitable in any entrepreneurial endeavours, so resilience and a high risk tolerance are vital.

Maintain a growth mindset where abilities can be developed through dedication and learning from failures. Every mistake provides an opportunity to improve. Stay persistent through challenges knowing that mastery comes from sustained effort. The only true failure is giving up on your vision too early.

Purpose Over Profit

It's easy to get caught up in the profit motives and potential financial rewards of self-employment. But only connecting your work to a higher purpose beyond monetary gains can provide motivation that profit alone cannot.

Focusing solely on profit puts you on a never-ending treadmill, constantly chasing the next business or revenue milestone. There is always more money to be made. Basing your self-worth and validation on profit metrics can lead to burnout and a lack of fulfilment.

On the other hand, when you align work with contributing value to society, helping others, or creating positive change, you tap into a renewable energy source. Finding meaning and purpose in your entrepreneurial contributions energizes you through inevitable ups and downs in a way profit motives cannot alone.

As Anita Roddick, founder of The Body Shop, wisely said: 'To succeed you have to believe in something with such a passion that it becomes a reality' (Veroniek Collewaert, 2016). It is this passion and purpose that can help weather external storms and challenges that may test a business focused solely on profits or validation.

Purpose also provides a North Star for decision-making when the path forward seems unclear. By staying grounded in your mission and values, difficulties can be viewed as opportunities to live out your purpose rather than threats.

Connecting your work to transformative purpose creates ripple effects that extend far beyond your bottom line. Pursuing positive change and making a difference energizes others as well.

With a purpose-driven mindset, progress is not just measured in dollars but human impact.

Managing the Psychological Challenges

The solopreneurial path is filled with emotional highs and lows. Without the structure of a corporate job, you must proactively manage common psychological hurdles that can derail progress.

Loneliness and Isolation

Working independently can take an emotional toll over time. Entrepreneurs often report feeling lonelier than traditional employees. Without the built-in social interactions and community of an office setting, it's easy to feel isolated and adrift when working solo.

After all, we are social creatures by nature. Without the daily in-person conversations with colleagues, the silence can chip away at motivation and inspiration. Facing challenges without personal support makes it harder to pick yourself back up after setbacks.

Actively nurturing personal relationships and seeking community are essential to avoid the pitfalls of isolation. On top of what we discussed in chapter five on Building Your Team, consider coworking spaces to get out of the house and gain camaraderie with fellow entrepreneurs.

Attend networking events both for business connections and social interactions. Set up regular video calls with mentors, peers, and friends to prevent loneliness from spiralling into depression.

Also make time for hobbies and social activities outside of work. Schedule meetups, join clubs related to your interests, and prioritize quality time with family and friends. Maintaining balance keeps your tank full.

While the flexibility of working for yourself is appealing, humans need connection. With some creativity and initiative, you can assemble your own 'team' of supporters, collaborators, and community that fills the social gap and enriches your entrepreneurial journey.

Working alone can take an emotional toll over time. Entrepreneurs often feel lonelier than traditional employees. Without daily social office interactions and a built-in community, it's easy to feel adrift.

Actively nurture personal relationships and seek community to avoid isolation. Attend networking events, join masterminds, and schedule regular social activities away from work. Coworking spaces can also provide camaraderie when working solo gets isolating.

Imposter Syndrome

Feeling like a fraud is common when stretching your abilities. Imposter syndrome manifests as self-doubt, discounting achievements and fear of being exposed. But have confidence in your vision and skills. As Michelle Obama said, 'One of the lessons that I grew up with was to always stay true to yourself and never let what somebody else says distract you from your goals. And so when I hear about negative and false attacks, I really don't invest any energy in them, because I know who I am' (Hutto, n.d.).

Here are some tips for overcoming imposter syndrome and building more confidence in your abilities as an entrepreneur:

- Recognize that self-doubt is common. Even the most successful entrepreneurs experience imposter syndrome at times. It doesn't mean you are a fraud.
- Celebrate and write down your wins and accomplishments, both big and small. Refer back to this when you are feeling like an imposter.
- Own your expertise. Don't diminish or downplay your skills and knowledge. You offer unique value.

- Remember that becoming comfortable with uncertainty and taking risks is part of the entrepreneurial journey. It's okay not to have all the answers right away.
- Focus on learning and progress rather than perfection. You don't have to be flawless to be valuable.
- Open up about your self-doubts to a trusted friend or mentor. Speaking about it can help release the grip of imposter thoughts.
- Visualize yourself succeeding. Imagine delivering an amazing pitch or product customers love before you have to actually do it.
- Watch your self-talk and challenge negative thoughts. Ask yourself, 'Would I say this about a friend?' and treat yourself with the same compassion.
- Take on challenges outside your comfort zone and upskill. This builds hard evidence of your expanding abilities.
- Remember that most people present confident personas outwardly, even if they have self-doubts inside. Don't compare your behind-the-scenes feelings to others' highlight reels.

With time and effort, you can move past the feelings of being an imposter and build unshakeable confidence in your worth and talents as an entrepreneur.

Comparison and Self-Criticism

It's tempting to measure your own entrepreneurial journey against the carefully curated highlights and successes you see others posting on social media and in the press. But comparing your daily struggles and behind-the-scenes efforts to the highlight reels of others is a recipe for discontent.

Seeing fellow entrepreneurs launching new products, speaking at conferences, or landing big interviews can trigger an unhealthy spiral of negative social comparison. Your inner critic takes over, making statements like:

- 'They already seem so much more successful than I am, even though we started around the same time.'
- 'I should be further along by now based on how well they are doing.'
- 'Maybe I don't have what it takes if progress is so hard for me but not for them.'

Once you start down this comparison rabbit hole, it breeds self-criticism, erodes confidence, and distorts your self-image. Your own achievements and progress seem inadequate through this distorted lens.

To break free of the comparison trap, remember that no entrepreneur's journey is free of challenges and self-doubt. Focus on your own definition of success rather than arbitrary outside standards. Avoid the temptation to judge your internal struggles against the external persona others portray.

Run your own race and define milestones that reflect your unique vision and goals. Social media is not an accurate benchmark for the winding road of entrepreneurship. With self-awareness and conscious effort, you can short-circuit the unhealthy comparison cycle and reframe setbacks as opportunities for growth. Your path may have more twists and turns, but the destination can be just as rewarding.

Cultivating Healthy Coping Strategies

A proactive self-care regimen helps manage the psychological ups and downs of entrepreneurship. Beyond commonly discussed tactics like meditation and establishing work-life balance, consider these additional strategies:

Get Outdoors and Move Your Body

Spending time outdoors and exercising provides proven mental health benefits while reducing stress. I've made regular exercise and outdoor time a cornerstone of my self-care regimen.

I attend BFT[1] training classes four days per week at 5.30 p.m. Monday through Thursday. Scheduling evening workouts forces me to step away from work and transition my mindset. Fridays I rest, while Saturday mornings I rise early for an 8.00 a.m. class.

Studies show consistent exercise increases energy, focus, and creativity due to endorphins and brain chemicals. A 2019 study in the *Journal of Affective Disorders* found that just twenty to thirty minutes of aerobic exercise significantly reduced stress hormone levels and elevated moods (Ida, 2019). So counterintuitively, taking time for fitness allows me greater mental acuity during working hours. My Sunday morning football team provides camaraderie and laughs.

I also try to spend every Friday working remotely from a local Starbucks. Simply changing my workspace for a day helps break the monotony of working from a home office. Being around the buzz of a coffee shop and having little interactions with baristas provides a mental refresh.

Beyond structured activities, simple actions like taking walking meetings, hiking on lunch breaks, or just sitting outdoors boost mood. Research confirms spending time in nature has measurable stress-reduction benefits (Franco, 2019).

Making movement and outdoor time daily habits provide a reset from pressures. Protecting physical and mental well-being allows you to better pursue your vision long-term. The grind is a marathon, not a sprint—self-care builds the endurance to go the distance.

---

[1] https://www.bodyfittraining.com/

Engage Your Creativity

It's easy to fixate solely on your business and grind away without any creative outlet. However, consistently channelling your creativity into hobbies and passions outside of work rejuvenates the spirit and avoids burnout.

In my free time I've recently started painting again after years away from the canvas. Though my paintings will never make it to the walls in my home, the process of mixing colours and trying to capture a scene is immensely satisfying.

I am also in the process of starting an informal podcast with friends as another creative outlet unrelated to work. Occasional YouTube videos allow me to scratch my video-editing itch in a low-pressure hobby environment.

These and other hobbies like writing, photography, or learning an instrument allow your mind to wander and make new connections freely. The structured focus and problem-solving of artistic pursuits provide a different satisfaction than business tasks.

Building something purely for your own enjoyment and sense of challenge, not for profit or external validation, taps into the playful innovative spirit that led you to entrepreneurship in the first place.

Schedule time for your creative outlets to ensure they don't get crowded out by business demands. The renewed mental clarity and passion will counterbalance any 'lost time' spent away from work.

Just as caring for your physical body is necessary to perform optimally, nourishing your innate creativity nourishes your soul. Maintaining hobbies prevents the human spirit from being confined to the mundane.

Practise Active Gratitude

Focusing on blessings counteracts our natural negativity bias. I make a point to take time each day to actively reflect on people, experiences, or accomplishments I'm grateful for. This ritual of counting my wins fuels resilience during difficult stretches.

I also use breathwork apps like Breathwrk[2] when I need to centre myself. Taking a few minutes to consciously breathe and clear my mind reduces anxiety and sharpens focus.

Studies show that practices like loving-kindness meditation elevate mood and reduce depression. When I'm feeling particularly down, I'll pick a random person and silently wish, 'May you be happy, may you be healthy, and may you be at peace.' A 2008 study in Motivation and Emotion found that just seven minutes of loving-kindness meditation increased positive emotions (Xianglong Zeng, 2015).

Writing daily positive affirmations in my morning journal reminds me of my strengths and worth. Affirming 'I am capable' or 'Challenges make me stronger' reinforces a growth mindset to start the day.

Little rituals of gratitude, breathwork, compassion, and positive affirmations counteract negativity bias. By making time for these practices, I nourish the inner resources to handle external challenges.

Incorporating research-backed coping mechanisms establishes a multifaceted self-care regimen. Be proactive about protecting your mental health as an entrepreneur—your mindset impacts your ability to turn vision into reality.

Sustaining Motivation and Drive

Maintaining motivation and drive as an entrepreneur is critical, yet inevitably ebbs and flows. The freedom of working for yourself can quickly turn to isolation without daily structure and accountability. The uncertainty of forging your own path

---

[2] https://www.breathwrk.com/

leads to frequent doubt. Milestones come slowly. Setbacks are disheartening.

It's easy to lose inspiration when the initial excitement of your vision fades under mundane business realities. Fatigue sets in. Confidence wavers. The passion that fuelled your launch can feel fleeting.

This makes intentionally designing your lifestyle to spark motivation essential. You must proactively kindle your inner fire daily through routines that promote clarity and progress.

Beyond commonly discussed tactics like surrounding yourself with a supportive community or tracking measurable wins, consider these additional strategies for sustaining your drive:

Listen to Podcasts in Related (or Unrelated) Domains

Exposing yourself to podcasts in complementary spaces fuels creativity by sparking new connections through what James Altucher calls 'idea sex' (Altucher, n.d.). Hearing fellow entrepreneurs openly share their journeys re-energizes my own.

Some podcasts I regularly tune into include *Acquired*, *The Tim Ferriss Show*, *Creator Science*, *Founders*, and *How I Write*. Listening to start-up founders, authors, and innovative leaders discuss their stories gets my creative juices flowing.

I also find enjoyment and motivation from shows unrelated to business like *Conan O'Brien Needs a Friend*, *Freakonomics Radio*, and *The Jordan Harbinger Show*. Allowing my mind to explore widely through podcasts often generates inspiration in unexpected ways.

Some of my favourites across various interests include *The Financial Coconut*, *Marketing Against the Grain*, *The Matt Walker Podcast*, *The Morgan Housel Podcast*, *Unconfuse Me with Bill Gates*, and *The Tony Robbins Podcast*.

The diversity of perspectives keeps me engaged. I may not always directly apply lessons but expanding my knowledge sparks creativity. Letting ideas freely intersect gets me thinking in new directions.

Carving out podcast listening time feels productive even when not 'working.' Exposing myself to fellow entrepreneurs and interesting thinkers energizes and inspires me to keep grinding.

Exposing yourself to podcasts in complementary spaces fuels creativity by sparking new connections. Hearing fellow entrepreneurs share their journeys re-energizes your own.

Learn a New Skill

Setting aside time for structured learning keeps your mind active and capabilities expanding as an entrepreneur. Consistently developing new skills generates motivation by driving progress.

I dedicate Wednesday afternoon and a daily thirty-minute reading block just after lunch every day to intentional learning. I might review saved YouTube tutorials on podcast editing or work through an online course on UI design. Recent skills I've focused on include copywriting, SEO optimization, video production, and user experience.

As brain coach Jim Kwik highlights in his book *Limitless* (Kwik, 2020), regular reading expands knowledge and boosts creativity by strengthening neural connections. Studies show reading promotes idea generation and an innovative mindset.

The process of honing new capabilities pushes me intellectually. Having a 'beginner's mindset' keeps me inspired by tapping into the excitement of growth and discovery.

Steven Lock saved thousands in web design fees by learning to build his coaching business' website himself. Acquiring new skills opens entrepreneurial possibilities.

Steve Jobs attributed his pioneering of personal computing to a calligraphy course he took purely out of curiosity years prior to founding Apple. You never know how developing an unrelated skill may prove surprisingly relevant over time.

Fighting stagnation by engaging in training regular skills keeps your entrepreneurial fire lit. Structure feeds motivation. You remain inspired while expanding the possibilities of what you can achieve.

Setting aside time for structured learning keeps your mind active and expands capabilities over time. Stay inspired by growing—avoid stagnation.

Making motivation a conscious daily priority rather than passive outcome is key. Trying new sparks, from podcasts to skills development, prevents the passion flame from being extinguished by entrepreneurial realities. With consistency, you can sustain the inspiration needed to turn vision into an enduring reality.

The self-employment journey is filled with exhilarating highs and gut-wrenching lows. You must proactively protect your emotional well-being to thrive through the inevitable ups and downs.

Accept uncertainty as part of the process. Progress won't follow a linear path. Reframe setbacks as opportunities for growth. Focus on celebrating small wins.

Counter isolation by intentionally cultivating community and relationships. Seek out mentorship, peer connections, and mastermind groups for support.

Address imposter syndrome through positive self-talk, visualization, and focusing on progress over perfection. Your doubts do not define you.

Limit unhealthy comparisons. Run your own race based on your authentic definition of success. Social media distorts reality.

Incorporate self-care practices like meditation, exercise, creativity, and gratitude rituals into your routine. These renew your energy reserves.

Structure lifestyle habits that spark inspiration day-to-day. Continuously expand your knowledge and skills. Consume diverse podcasts and books.

The emotional rollercoaster of entrepreneurship intensifies everything. But with self-compassion, resilience, and community, you will thrive.

You now have strategies for managing the psychological challenges that accompany charting your own course. Stay grounded in purpose. The freedom ahead is worth weathering the turbulence.

Key Takeaways

- Accept uncertainty as inherent to entrepreneurship. Progress won't be linear, so celebrate small wins and view setbacks as learning opportunities.

- Proactively address loneliness and isolation that comes from solo work through community building, relationships, mentorship, and peer connections for support.

- Manage imposter syndrome by focusing on growth over perfection, positive self-talk, and acknowledging doubts are normal but don't define your abilities.

- Avoid unhealthy social comparisons by benchmarking your progress against your goals rather than distorted perceptions of others' highlights on social media.

- Incorporate consistent self-care practices like meditation, exercise, hobbies, gratitude rituals, and learning to renew energy reserves and spark daily motivation through challenging times.

Conclusion

The Takeaway Treasure Chest:
Key Lessons Learned

Most of us would have heard of Alice in Wonderland (Wikipedia, n.d.). It is one of my favourite movies and probably not for the reasons you are thinking.

For those of you who may be unfamiliar, the story is about Alice returning to the magical world from her childhood adventure, where she reunites with her old friends and learns of her true destiny: to end the Red Queen's reign of terror. Along the way, she faces many challenges and dangers, such as the Jabberwocky, the Bandersnatch, and the Red Queen's army.

She also meets new characters, such as the Mad Hatter, the White Queen, and the Cheshire Cat. Through her journey, Alice discovers her courage, her identity, and her power to change the world. She also realizes that she does not have to conform to the expectations of others, but can follow her own dreams and passions.

There are many parallels between Alice's journey and my self-employment journey, which you may also find relevant.

The Power of Perseverance

I had a good work buddy during my first job at the telco's call centre. Desmond is a few years my senior, is really funny, and was my main motivation to further my studies. He also shared with me that he was looking out for other jobs because he cannot take stress. Getting nasty calls from customers on a daily basis can be stressful no matter how used to it you are.

Because of that, he deliberately chose to work in the healthcare department and specifically in the Medical Records Office because records retrieval did not sound stressful at all.

I snickered when I found out he finally joined the industry and department of his choice. How could someone with a few more years of life experience be so susceptible to work stress?

Before my snicker even wore off, I encountered my version of stress and it came bouts after bouts as I made all the schoolboy mistakes in my first business. From inability to make payroll and rent due to poor business management, to business winter due to the 2007 Global Financial Crisis, to pressure from subsequent shareholders that affected my daily sleep and often made me wake up in cold sweat. Not to mention the occasional people conflict management that I just found so hard and unappealing to deal with.

Through a combination of dumb luck and the lack of a better option, I clung on. As much as I don't look forward to it and often procrastinate the hell out of it before I begin, I dug deep and faced the discomfort head on.

Financially I'm glad I hung on because I managed to get a good payout when I decided to sell my shares to other shareholders. That would not have happened had I given up at any point when a pin dropped. Importantly, the experience gained was life-changing. From someone who only did the bare minimum as an employee, I am forced to step up and step into shoes larger than I can fill just so we can make sure the business survives.

And survived it did. It even thrived at one point. It could have ended better but as Loki shared with Thanos in *Avengers: Infinity War*: 'I consider experience as experience.'[1]

---

[1] https://www.imdb.com/title/tt4154756/characters/nm1089991

Start with Quitting

I'm on my sixth business and second solopreneur journey but all this (including this book) would likely not have happened if I did not quit my last job.

Leadership Coach Sarah Weiler talked about this in a TEDx talk 'Knowing When to Quit' (Weiler, 2018). She was formerly a teacher and was constantly unhappy and stressed out. Quitting that job finally was the best decision she ever made, and it opened up new opportunities and possibilities for her.

She added that quitting is often seen as a sign of weakness, failure of lack of commitment, but quitting can also be a positive and empowering choice, especially when something is not working for us or serving us well.

Because we are so ingrained to focus on the 'sunk costs fallacy'—the tendency to continue investing in something that is not giving us the desired results, just because we have already invested a lot of time, money, or energy into it. This fallacy can trap us in situations that are harmful to our well-being, such as toxic relationships, unfulfilling jobs, or unrealistic dreams.

I had my fair share of sunk cost fallacy in my last job. The title was great, the scope was what I was dreaming of and I can almost guarantee that I would not be retrenched since it is quasi-government.

There were things that I had to give up to fit into the role. Things that included my values, my opinions, and my independence. Asking yourself what the cost of staying is, the benefit of leaving, and what is stopping you from leaving would help give you better clarity to your current employment situation, which may be driving you nuts.

Quitting can be a positive and courageous act. Learn to trust your intuition and feelings when you think it is time to part ways. In doing so, you could start the new chapter to happiness, health, and authenticity in your lives.

Cultivating Gratitude

As much as there are downsides and risks involved in self-employment, there are a lot more upsides and gains. Famous solopreneur Justin Welsh built a portfolio of his one-person business to US$5 million with a combination of digital courses, coaching and consulting, affiliate marketing, sponsorships and partnerships, as well as speaking and hosting (Welsh, X, 2023).

Since there is no company to cap your earnings in the form of a salary or commission structure, there is no limit to your earning power if that is what you are optimizing for.

Justin is also married but childless by design. For any parents out there, especially those with young children, you would know you don't have as many hours as someone who doesn't have children.

Randi Zuckerberg, the founder and CEO of Zuckerberg Media and the sister of Meta founder, Mark Zuckerberg, is often quoted for saying 'work, sleep, family, fitness, or friends: pick three' (Stillman, 2016). The implication is that it is impossible to have a balanced life and that one has to sacrifice some aspects of their well-being to achieve success in others.

Although many have criticized this as a false dilemma and that one can have more than three things in their life if they manage their time well, it is a reflection that we only have twenty-four hours a day and there can ultimately only be so many pieces of pie.

In the self-employment journey, it is tempting to just keep chasing the dragon and max out your earning potential. But optimizing just for that would completely ignore the other merits it comes with, such as independence, freedom, and the ability to express creativity.

It is equally tempting to constantly compare ourselves with more successful people. I only make a fraction of what Justin is making. But I also have lovely children to care for, other solopreneur friends to hang out with over weekdays, and the freedom to flex my creative muscles in sound and video editing even though they make zero money.

Ultimately it is about the attitude of gratitude to acquire during this entire journey. There will be successes and challenges on this journey, which is often a lonely one. Being grateful for all that comes through regardless of whether you sent out the invite is key to happiness and fulfilment.

Every morning I start my day by journaling in the 5 Minute Journal, an app mentioned by Tim Ferriss in a podcast episode. As the name implies you jot down things three things that you are grateful for, what you hope to achieve that day, and a self-affirmation. In the evening, I would complete the day's entry by entering three great things that happened to me. Occasionally I would include how the day could have been better.

These keep me grounded and allow me to face every day with a smile on my face.

Ongoing Learning and Growth

At a session during an HR event, the speaker shared an analogy that involved his trip to the dentist.

The dentist asked if he brushed twice a day. He nodded yes. The dentist then asked if he flosses every tooth every day.

The speaker replied, occasionally but only selected teeth. He then asked the dentist if it is important to floss every tooth.

The dentist responded: 'Oh, only the ones you wish to keep.'

Just like regular car maintenance to prevent your car from breaking down on the highway, there are 'maintenance' steps that self-employed folks like you and me need to do to stay up to date.

I put up a LinkedIn post recently that went viral. In it, I mentioned that 'if you think lifelong learning is hard, try irrelevance and unemployment . . .'

For many working professionals, this constant OS upgrade does not come naturally. Especially for my generation (Gen X), we have been conditioned to think that you are done with all the learnings once you step out of university. In an era where life is slower and less competitive due to globalization, that is true.

You can be the number one in the small pond you call home country. But as country borders rescinded with the aid of internet, the small, isolated ponds slowly combined into one big sea. Without constant learning and upgrading, it is easy to be made obsolete.

Jim Kwik wrote in *Limitless* that 'reading is one of the best ways to upgrade your brain and unlock your exceptional life (Kwik, 2020). Reading not only improves your knowledge, vocabulary, creativity, and memory, but also boosts your focus, concentration, and self-discipline. Reading a bit every day can help you develop a consistent habit that will serve you well in all areas of your life. Reading is like exercise for your mind. It strengthens your mental muscles and keeps them in shape. Reading also reduces stress, enhances empathy, and increases happiness. Reading is a powerful tool that can transform your life for the better.'

Similar to the benefits one gets when you raise your daily heartrate through exercise, Jim Kwik suggests a daily diet of reading for at least thirty minutes a day to exercise your brain muscle.

Daily reading also has another benefit and that is you are training your brain to stay off your phone as you're training to maintain focus for a longer time on a singular task. According to Gloria Mark, PhD, our attention spans are shrinking. Her research shows that people average forty-seven seconds on any screen (American Psychological Association, 2023).

You might not care if your life is an endless scroll, but your body and mind keep score. Research suggests that the less you focus, the more likely you are to experience stress and anxiety and have a harder time being present and feeling happy.

As with all things, I time-blocked reading into my calendar. It currently sits as a thirty-minute block just after lunch so that would be me chilling while reading as I ease myself back to work.

Beyond reading, I also keep myself up to date with several newsletter subscriptions that are relevant to my work or just things I believe are interesting developments. These include a bunch on marketing, productivity/motivational, and AI.

Here are some of my top picks you may consider:

Marketing

- Neil Patel[2]
- The Marketing Millennials[3]
- Justin Welsh[4]

Productivity/Motivational

- Ali Abdaal[5]
- More To That[6]
- Arnold's Pump Club[7]

AI

- AI Vibes[8]
- Prompt Engineering Daily[9]
- Future AI Lab[10]

Setting longer time aside for structured learning is also important as what you get in a newsletter or a LinkedIn post could be sorely out of context.

---

[2] https://neilpatel.com/

[3] https://www.thedanielmurray.com/themarketingmillennials

[4] https://www.justinwelsh.me/

[5] https://aliabdaal.com/

[6] https://moretothat.com/

[7] https://arnoldspumpclub.com/

[8] https://www.aiwithvibes.com/

[9] https://www.neatprompts.com/

[10] https://futureailab.com/

There are plenty of online courses you can consider on the internet and you don't have to overthink it. Consider the one that appeals to you the most and you don't have to complete it if you see no value mid-way through.

I set aside two hours a week on this and so far have completed courses on remote work, podcasting, LinkedIn growth, notion, writing, and many more. As of this writing, I am halfway through a course on sound design. I have no idea when this will come in useful but I became very fascinated with sound design since I started podcasting.

But I will always think back to what Steve Jobs said that you can only connect the dots looking backwards (Stanford, 2008). He was referring to the idea that life is unpredictable and you cannot always plan your future based on your present situation. You have to trust that the choices you make and the experiences you have will somehow lead you to your desired destination, even if you don't see it clearly at the moment.

He explained how dropping out of college, getting fired from Apple, and being diagnosed with cancer were all dots that connected him to his success and happiness later on. He said that dropping out of college allowed him to take classes that he was interested in, such as calligraphy, which influenced the design of the Macintosh computer. He said that getting fired from Apple gave him the opportunity to start new ventures, such as Pixar and NeXT, which eventually led him back to Apple. He said that being diagnosed with cancer made him realize what was truly important in life and motivated him to pursue his passion and vision.

He concluded his speech by saying: 'You have to trust in something—your gut, destiny, life, karma, whatever. This approach has never let me down, and it has made all the difference in my life.'

May that approach also make all the difference in your life as you pivot from mid-career to self-employment.

Acknowledgements

To Nora Nazerene Abu Bakar, my Penguin Random House publisher: For believing in my ramblings before they even had a title. I owe you a lifetime of coffee.

To Amberdawn Manaois: For turning my messy word salad into something shiny and readable. You're the magic touch that made me sound (almost) like a real writer.

To my incredible friends: For sharing your self-employment adventures and proving I'm not alone in this crazy ride. You are the fuel that kept this book going.

Everyone I've crossed paths with: You are the tapestry of my life, the good, the bad, and everything in between. Thank you for teaching me and making this journey an adventure.

To my family: Thanks for constantly asking, 'When are you getting a real job?' Your nagging was the push I needed to finally prove I could (sort of) make a living off self-employment (and hopefully more from this book). Maybe now I can afford to buy you all matching 'World's Best Author's Family' mugs. You're welcome!

References

Adney, I. (n.d.). *Why this creator left the corporate world and became a storyteller.* Retrieved from ConvertKit Blog: https://convertkit.com/resources/creator-stories/lawrence-yeo

Altucher, J. (n.d.). *The Ultimate Guide for Becoming an Idea Machine.* Retrieved from James Altucher Blog: https://jamesaltucher.com/blog/the-ultimate-guide-for-becoming-an-idea-machine/

American Psychological Association. (2023, February). *Speaking of Psychology: Why our attention spans are shrinking, with Gloria Mark, PhD.* Retrieved from American Psychological Association: https://www.apa.org/news/podcasts/speaking-of-psychology/attention-spans

Anna Katharina Schaffner, P. (2020, September 16). *Perseverance in Psychology: Meaning, Importance & Books.* Retrieved from PositivePsychology.com: https://positivepsychology.com/perseverance/

Baer, D. (2013, May 17). *How LinkedIn's Reid Hoffman Jumped Off A Cliff And Built An Airplane.* Retrieved from Fast Company: https://www.fastcompany.com/3009831/how-linkedins-reid-hoffman-jumped-off-a-cliff-and-built-an-airplane

Bezos, J. (2017, August). *Regret Minimization.* (A. Winkler, Interviewer) Retrieved from https://open.spotify.com/episode/4AeSPoEjmfMUNvdIt50tTs?si=48f36332b8394353

Bill Walsh, S. J. (2010). *The Score Takes Care of Itself: My Philosophy of Leadership.* Portfolio.

Britny Kutuchief, T. R. (2023, March 27). *Best Time to Post on Social Media in 2024 [ALL NETWORKS].* Retrieved from Hootsuite Blog: https://blog.hootsuite.com/best-time-to-post-on-social-media/

Burkc, S. (2021, December 27). *Entrepreneurial Persistence: The Key To Success.* Retrieved from *Forbes*: https://www.forbes.com/sites/forbesbusinesscouncil/2021/12/27/entrepreneurial-persistence-the-key-to-success/?sh=753da630232d

Chan, J. (n.d.). *Find Your Superpower with Juliana Chan.* Retrieved from www.julianachan.org/courses

Cigna. (2022). *Global Well-Being Survey: Singapore Insights Report.*

Clarkson, N. (2015, December 9). *Richard Branson: Why delegation is crucial to success.* Retrieved from Virgin Blog: https://www.virgin.com/about-virgin/latest/richard-branson-why-delegation-crucial-success

Clear, J. (2018). Chapter 13: How to Stop Procrastinating by Using the Two-Minute Rule. In J. Clear, *Atomic Habits.* Avery.

CollectiveContent. (2016, October 28). *Andrew Davis on: Content . . . relationships . . . trust . . . success.* Retrieved from CollectiveContent Blog: https://collectivecontent.agency/2016/10/28/andrew-davis-content-relationships-trust-success/

Comings, J. (2007). *Persistence: Helping Adult Education Students Reach Their Goals.* National Center for the Study of Adult Learning and Literacy, 23: https://www.ncsall.net/fileadmin/resources/ann_rev/comings-02.pdf

Covey, S. R. (2020). *The 7 Habits of Highly Effective People.* Simon & Schuster.

Design Better. (2022, July). *Seth Godin, Rewind: Learning to take risks, be generous, and make a ruckus.* Retrieved from Spotify: https://open.spotify.com/episode/25ThKckFjrkMkXNOGg8gg1?si=30dea86226824427

Dr Mike Wilmot, D. O. (2019, November 6). *Conscientiousness is top personality predictor of positive career and work-related outcomes, has broad benefits.* Retrieved from: https://twin-cities.umn.edu/news-events/conscientiousness-top-personality-predictor-positive-career-and-work-related-outcomes

Engineers.SG. (2015, May 21). *Adrian Tan - Fuckup Nights - Singapore, Vol. II.* Retrieved from YouTube: https://youtu.be/LIvQrGHZiCQ?si=tT6Hr_r2a1dnWp0f

Eyal, N. (2019). *Indistractable: How to Control Your Attention and Choose Your Life.* Bloomsbury.

Eyal, N. (n.d.). *Free Schedule Maker: a Google Sheet to Plan Your Week.* Retrieved from Nir And Far: https://www.nirandfar.com/schedule-maker/

Ferriss, T. (2016). *Tools Of Titans: The Tactics, Routines, and Habits of Billionaires, Icons, and World-Class Performers.* Houghton Mifflin Harcourt.

Ferriss, T. (2017, April). *Why you should define your fears instead of your goals.* Retrieved from TED: https://www.ted.com/talks/tim_ferriss_why_you_should_define_your_fears_instead_of_your_goals

Ferriss, T. (2022, January 12). Retrieved from X: https://twitter.com/tferriss/status/1481318414824218632?lang=en

Ferriss, T. (2023, September 28). *Shane Parrish on Wisdom from Warren Buffett, Rules for Better Thinking, How to Reduce Blind Spots, The Dangers of Mental Models, and More (#695).* Retrieved from The Tim Ferriss Show: https://tim.blog/2023/09/28/shane-parrish-farnam-street/

Franco, L. S., Shanahan, D. F., and Fuller, R. A. (2019). *Urban nature experiences reduce stress in the context of daily life based on salivary biomarkers.* Retrieved from Frontiers in Psychology, 10, 722.

Fuller, R. B. (1970). *I Seem To Be a Verb.* Bantam Books.

Gallup. (2017). *State of the Americna Manager: Analytics and Advice for Leaders.*

Gallup. (n.d.). *CliftonStrengths*. Retrieved from https://www.gallup.com/cliftonstrengths/en/home.aspx

Gerber, M. E. (2004). *The E-Myth Revisited: Why Most Small Businesses Don't Work and What to Do About It.* Harper Business.

Godin, S. (1999). *Permission Marketing: Turning Strangers into Friends and Friends into Customers.* Simon & Schuster.

Hick, W. E. (1952). *On the rate of gain of information.* Retrieved from *Quarterly Journal of Experimental Psychology*, 11–26.

Hutto, C. (2024, Feb 21). *32 Powerful & Empowering Michelle Obama Quotes.* Retrieved from InHerSight: https://www.inhersight.com/blog/women-to-know/michelle-obama-quotes

Ibrahim, W. (2021, May 8). *Jeff Bezos uses a simple framework for making big decisions. Here's how it works.* Retrieved from Fast Company: https://www.fastcompany.com/90662406/jeff-bezos-uses-a-simple-framework-for-making-big-decisions-heres-how-it-works

Ida, Hiroshi, Masahiro Doi, Masahiro Nakagawa, Masahiro Nakagawa, Masahiro Nakagawa, and Masahiro Nakagawa. *Acute Effects of Aerobic Exercise on Salivary Free Cortisol and Subjective Depressive Symptoms in Patients with Major Depressive Disorder.* Retrieved from *Journal of Affective Disorders* 251 (2019): 233–237.

IMDb. (2018). *Avengers: Infinity War - Tom Hiddleston: Loki.* Retrieved from IMDb: https://www.imdb.com/title/tt4154756/characters/nm1089991

Isaacson, W. (2011). *Steve Jobs: A Biography.* Simon & Schuster.

Joseph P. Lash, T. L. (1997). *Helen and Teacher the Story of Helen Keller and Anne Sullivan Macy.* Da Capo Press.

Juita, R. (2023, October). Retrieved from LinkedIn: https://www.linkedin.com/feed/update/urn:li:activity:7104995400524185600?updateEntityUrn=urn%3Ali%3Afs_feedUpdate%3A%28V2%2Curn%3Ali%3Aactivity%3A7104995400524185600%29

Kagan, N. (n.d.). *Noah Kagan Podcast.* Retrieved from Noah Kagan: https://noahkagan.com/podcast/

Kelvin Learns Investing. (n.d.). *Kelvin Learns Investing.* Retrieved from YouTube: https://www.youtube.com/c/kelvinlearnsinvesting

Knight, P. (2016). *Shoe Dog: A Memoir by the Creator of Nike.* Scribner.

Kwik, J. (2020). *Limitless: Upgrade Your Brain, Learn Anything Faster, and Unlock Your Exceptional Life.* Hay House Inc.

Lai, N. (2023, Sep 8). (A. Tan, Interviewer)

Lock, S. (2023, September 22). Interview. (A. Tan, Interviewer)

Maraboli, D. S. (2013). *Unapologetically You: Reflections on Life and the Human Experience.* Better Today.

Mewborn, A. (n.d.). *Steal The EXACT LinkedIn Strategy That 5X'd My Inbound Leads In 9 Months!* Retrieved from Brand30: https://www.brand30.io/free-linkedin-training

Multiple. (n.d.). *Fractional work.* Retrieved from Wikipedia: https://en.wikipedia.org/wiki/Fractional_work

Newport, C. (2016). *Deep Work: Rules for Focused Success in a Distracted World.* Grand Central Publishing.

Newport, C. (2016). *So Good They Can't Ignore You.* Grand Central Publishing.

Ng, J. (2022, June). 95: Prudential Jaslyn Ng on rejecting a $250k package as Global HR Director and her leap into the insurance sector. (A. Tan, Interviewer)

Nohria, M. E. (2018, July-August). *How CEOs Manage Time.* Retrieved from Harvard Business Review: https://hbr.org/2018/07/how-ceos-manage-time

Nucleus_AI. (2023, May 24). *The Biggest Risk is not Taking Any Risk.* Retrieved from YourStory: https://yourstory.com/2023/05/embracing-risk-zuckerbergs-philosophy

Pang, A. T. (2013). *Everything you wish to ask a headhunter.* Singapore: Candid Creation Publishing.

Partaker, E. (2020). *The 3 Alarms: A Simple System to Transform Your Health, Wealth, and Relationships Forever.* Bowker.

Pradeepa, S. (2023, September 5). *Why Persistence is Important: 8 Benefits & 6 Ways to Develop.* Retrieved from Believe

In Mind: https://www.believeinmind.com/self-growth/why-persistence-is-important/

Rao, S. (2017, September 26). *How Writing 1000 Words a Day Changed my Life*. Retrieved from Medium: https://medium.com/the-mission/how-writing-1000-words-a-day-changed-my-life-cf72453b8fef

Raymond Hull, D. L. (1976). *The Peter Principle: Why Things Always Go Wrong*. Bantam book. Originally published in 1969.

Robbins, M. (2017). *The 5 Second Rule*. Mel Robbins Productions Inc.

Rober, M. (2023, June 10). *I Gave the 2023 MIT Commencement Speech*. Retrieved from YouTube: https://www.youtube.com/watch?v=1UTjWy-vnOo

Roy, P. (2022, December 23). *How Many Times Thomas Failed? Know Edison's Marvellous and Lesser Known Inventions*. Retrieved from Vedantu: https://www.vedantu.com/blog/how-many-times-edison-failed-to-invent-bulb

Ryan, E. (2023, May 24). *Growth Mindset Vs Fixed Mindset: What Do They Really Mean?* Retrieved from Mentorloop: https://mentorloop.com/blog/growth-mindset-vs-fixed-mindset-what-do-they-really-mean/

Schmidt, A. (2023, Aug 10). (A. Tan, Interviewer)

Schwartz, B. (2020, May). *What role does luck play in your life?* Retrieved from TED: https://www.ted.com/talks/barry_schwartz_what_role_does_luck_play_in_your_life?language=en

Seek, S. (n.d.). *Steven Seek LinkedIn*. Retrieved from LinkedIn: https://www.linkedin.com/in/stevenseek/

Shankar, S. S. (2021). *Celebrating Silence*. Jaico Publishing House.

Sivers, D. (2022). *Anything You Want: 40 lessons for a new kind of entrepreneur*. Hit Media.

Stahl, S. (2021, October 13). *12th Annual B2B Content Marketing: Benchmarks, Budgets, and Trends*. Retrieved from Content

Marketing Institute: https://contentmarketinginstitute.com/
articles/b2b-power-content-marketing-research/

Stanford. (2008, May 15). *Steve Jobs' 2005 Stanford Commencement Address (with intro by President John Hennessy)*. Retrieved from YouTube: https://youtu.be/Hd_ptbiPoXM?si=jADa4CkSkMfv3e26

Statista. (n.d.). *Podcast Advertising - Worldwide*. Retrieved from Statista: https://www.statista.com/outlook/dmo/digital-media/digital-music/podcast-advertising/worldwide

Stillman, J. (2016, February 3). *Work, Sleep, Family, Fitness, or Friends: Pick 3*. Retrieved from Inc: https://www.inc.com/jessica-stillman/work-sleep-family-fitness-or-friends-pick-3.html

Studer, Q. (2018, June 30). *Studer: Show me your calendar, and I'll tell you your priorities*. Retrieved from *Pensacola News Journal:* https://www.pnj.com/story/money/2018/06/30/studer-show-me-your-calendar-and-ill-tell-you-your-priorities/744079002/

Tan, A. (2023, May 4). *Commentary: Should you take time off for leisure during working hours?* Retrieved from Channel NewsAsia: https://www.channelnewsasia.com/commentary/remote-work-home-afternoon-fun-time-leisure-employer-company-3461311

Tan, E. (2023, September 18). Interview. (A. Tan, Interviewer)

The Financial Coconut. (n.d.). *The Financial Coconut Podcast*. Retrieved from Spotify: https://open.spotify.com/show/6ndJZx2bk8jYgQHAXIwg1C?si=cda0a3ed35604bb4

Tiah, A. (2023, August 14). Interview. (A. Tan, Interviewer)

Toastmasters Club of Singapore. (n.d.). *TMCS Entrepreneur Club*. Retrieved from Toastmasters Singapore: https://toastmasters.org.sg/entrepreneur-club/

Veroniek Collewaert, F. A. (2016, June 16). *How Entrepreneurs Can Keep Their Passion from Fading*. Retrieved from Harvard Business Review: https://hbr.org/2016/06/how-entrepreneurs-can-keep-their-passion-from-fading

We Are Social, Hootsuite. (2021, January 27). *Digital 2021: Global Overview Report.* Retrieved from DataReportal: https://datareportal.com/reports/digital-2021-global-overview-report

Weiler, S. (2018, March 21). *Knowing when to quit | Sarah Weiler | TEDxNewham.* Retrieved from YouTube: https://www.youtube.com/watch?v=WWtRied_Tsk

Welsh, J. (n.d.). Retrieved from LinkedIn: https://www.linkedin.com/posts/justinwelsh_my-daily-routine-is-unbeatable-i-wake-up-activity-7134756291150786560-IzH1?utm_source=share&utm_medium=member_desktop

Welsh, J. (2023, October 30). Retrieved from X: https://twitter.com/thejustinwelsh/status/1718965233761329541

Wikipedia. (n.d.). *Alice in Wonderland (2010 film).* Retrieved from Wikipedia: https://en.wikipedia.org/wiki/Alice_in_Wonderland_(2010_film)

World Athletics. (2020, April 10). *10 of the greatest athletics examples of perseverance.* Retrieved from World Athletics: https://worldathletics.org/news/series/athletics-examples-of-perseverance

Xianglong Zeng, C. P. (2015, November 3). *The effect of loving-kindness meditation on positive emotions: a meta-analytic review.* Retrieved from Frontiers in Psychology: https://www.frontiersin.org/articles/10.3389/fpsyg.2015.01693/full

Yongfook, J. (n.d.). *A Bootstrapped SaaS Journey to $10K MRR.* Retrieved from Bannerbear: https://www.bannerbear.com/journey-to-10k-mrr/